∞

Our Arms

held

Cardboard and Sleeping bags

By Stacey Hessler

Copyright 2015

∞

∞

Part 1

The Occupation

∞

∞

"Organize, agitate, educate, must be our war cry" Susan B. Anthony

∞

It all started with a post on facebook. Students occupying wall St.! What is this about I thought? And what I thought was; my radical friends posting some insignificant occupation, confused and disbelieving the information, not really able to make sense of it, I ignored it, paid no attention, only a few radical postings. How important could this be? Why are they making such a big deal about nothing, nothing worth mentioning? Why are they making such a big deal about the media not being there? If it were important the media would cover it, I thought too. I blew it off as a too radical, less important, non-issue.

Yet every day I kept on seeing posts. What is this, what is this, what is going on, why is the media still not there? Still it was my "radical friends", as even I thought of them. After about day seven I started seeing some media coverage and more people posting about it. Even though I tried to pay no attention, to ignore it, I was still curious, still interested, it was something I didn't understand, but I wanted to. I started to look into this thing called Occupy Wall Street. What was it? Why are they there? What is it about? I couldn't find much.

Watching YouTube videos I started to become more than interested. Seeing it live, practically, the workings laid out in front of the screen. Occupying a space for a protest was such an interesting idea and once I started I could not stop trying to gather more and more information. I couldn't get it out of my mind. Soaking all this up I was constantly thinking "I want to be part of this, People Uniting".

The Occupy Wall Street website showed the park, the people's library, the people's tobacco table, the people's kitchen, comfort; the people's closet. You could feed your mind, your tobacco addiction, your belly, get supplies you needed. The people's library had librarians taking care of the books, the people's tobacco table, guys and girls sitting at the table rolling cigarettes, giving them away, the people's kitchen making food, feeding whomever was there, comfort with sleeping bags, warm clothes, toothpaste, tampons. Anything one would need was there, everyone volunteering, donating their time and supplies.

Marching to Wall Street day after day, drummers keeping the beat, cardboard signs, people's faces, their stories of why they were there, different people from all different places, all walks of life, all ages, coming together, uniting to change the world.

I decided I had to go, I had to travel, I had to spend my hard earned school savings to take the train and Occupy Wall Street. I didn't know what to expect, what I would find, what would happen to me, I just knew I had to take the leap of faith, I had to try, I want a better world, I want a government who listens to the people. This could be the change I had hoped for when I elected Obama. I had thought Obama would be the people's president, yet he did not meet my expectations. His time was up for me thinking he would change the world. His message of hope sank in my heart. He was not the answer I thought he would have been.

This seemed to be the people's movement, the people's way of rising up and being heard by this government. As I looked up the word occupy on facebook occupation after occupation popped up.

Occupy Florida, Occupy Orlando, Occupy Boston, Occupy London, Occupy, Occupy, and endless Occupy. This thing had blown up overnight. This was bigger than Wall Street, but Wall Street is where it all began. I had to go and check it out, I had to learn, learn what this was all about first hand, even though I had not an idea where or how, first hand was the only way. One week to learn and take home the information, the experience.

I would meet like minds, even though I was afraid, I would be alright. The time is now, if I want to help make change happen, I can't wait, the time is now for action. I want to be one of those people who will take action, who will be the change they wish to see in the world, if not me then who? How could I expect someone else to do it when I can do it myself? I must take action. Now is when the movement is happening. There is no other time to get involved. This is a chance to participate, to work for long term change in government. When people rise up in numbers to fight with their voices and bodies in protest of what is happening, in great numbers they hear us. In great numbers they see us. Only in great numbers, or else we are invisible. The 99% invisible, not seen, not heard.

I am willing to do this; I have a natural drive and motivation to do so. I have been motivated by all great movement leaders before me, Martin Luther King Jr., Gandhi, Malcolm X, Harriett Tubman, Helen Keller, Albert Einstein, Abraham Lincoln, Oprah Winfrey, Maya Angelou, John Lennon, Bob Marley, and none in this order. I thought about the movements in the past and how my whole life I knew if I had been alive then I would have wanted to be one of those few standing up and now I had that chance, I had to live my beliefs, I couldn't ignore this opportunity, on my way to deciding if I should go to Occupy Wall Street, I looked up Martin Luther King's speeches and played them, listened to them, read the words and all he is saying rings true in this time too. I have to believe that we can make a better world for our children. We are taking this world and its resources; we are poisoning our sky, sea, land, food, water. Companies are making all the laws with their lobbying and campaign funding, they are destroying the world and poisoning the people, risking future generations and we are silent. I will be silent no more. We make less and less, prices go up an up, people are losing their jobs, losing their houses, losing their cars, losing their health insurance, losing their retirement and we are silent. That's only the start, Unions are being destroyed, and people losing their jobs to corporations gone overseas, most of our goods are made in China. The American flag is made in China! College students can't find jobs and can't pay back loans, war, unemployment at 10%, did I mention enough about unemployment already, while banks and financial institutions get billions of dollars.

∞

We are disconnected and plugged in.

∞

This is no future to leave to my children, to leave to anyone's children. Wake up!

∞

"The need for change bulldozed a road down the center of my mind" Maya Angelou

∞

So I was ready for a train ride. I bought my ticket right at the DeLand train station on the day of my departure, not planning too far ahead. It was a Sunday, only the day before did I decide on it after talking to everyone in the family about wanting to go and it wasn't something I could plan in the future, for it was a now sort of thing. So Curtiss dropped me off at the train station with my backpack carefully packed with everything I would need inside of it, a bag with some food, a sleeping bag and my heavy jacket and I was off. I had checked the times of the train so I knew when I would need to be there and I got there with plenty of time to spare.

I went up to the window and bought my ticket to NYC and back home again, I figured if I decided to change it later I always could, but I had my way there and home, I didn't have to worry, not that I was planning on changing anything, but somewhere in the back of my mind I was keeping the possibility open, not knowing at all what to expect in any way, shape, or form. I was just doing it, taking one step at a time, just one step in front of the other.

∞

"They can not see that we have to lay one brick at a time, take one step at a time" Dorothy Day.

∞

I didn't realize until after I got the ticket that the train was delayed for four hours, I sure did get there with plenty of time to spare. So there I was waiting in this old train station, built when trains were a main form of transportation. It's small with long wooden benches to sit on. Outside there is a long overhang with fancy wood carvings around the edges, bricks line the walk. Another long wooden bench sits outside.

The kids and I on occasion have come to the train station to park and then walk along the tracks as far as we want to go and then we turn around and walk back. We walk along the tracks to see what we can spy, we always find discarded pieces of track along the banks of it, big fat rusted nails, rotted pieces of track, big brackets. We would carry what we could or wanted to individually haul back. Most of it we carried for a while looking at it and how it gets put together on the track and when we got tired of carrying it, we would leave it

11

along the side, metal is heavy, but some of the souvenirs made their way home and we still have some scattered around the house.

Lost in my mind only about 10 minutes had passed, I had so much time and Jeanie who is my best friend is so close to the train station I called her up and prayed she would answer so I could see her before I left, I could kill two birds with one stone, it would help pass the time rather than sit in this train station for four hours. Miracle of miracles she answered and miracle of miracles even still, even though the much dreaded Bill was home she came and picked me up anyway. So happy was I to see my friend and have some time to hang out, catch up, and smoke some for it had been a while for all.

I was glad to be going on this adventure and I was glad to have a kickoff to the adventure being at Jeanie's. We drank some coffee and even though a vegan I had to put a little cream in it because I did not like black coffee and she never had any soy, rice, or almond milk. I just put a drop, just to lighten it, just the least bit, I could splash in to give the illusion of cream but keep my 98% vegan status, and some sugar to sweeten it up. While

Jeanie ironed her clothes, we talked, her shadow for the next few hours talking in the laundry room, to the kitchen and back every once in a while for a refill of coffee and then it was time to head back to the train station to catch the train, I wanted to be there with plenty of time before the train was scheduled, so I was sure not to miss it, so Jeanie drove me back, we said our good-bye's, I grabbed my bags out of the car and headed into the train station to find it even further delayed so I still had waiting time. I was very excited and just wanted to get on the train already so I knew I was on my way to NY and Occupy Wall Street, hours later I was still in DeLand, no closer, but with a ticket, if only the train would come, I was so anxious to be on my way, as the train pulled up I was more than ready to get on by myself, all alone, not knowing what I would come across, just taking that first step into the unknown, standing there ready, waiting to board, I just wanted to get on the train so I would know I was on my way, and then I was and we were pulling away.

I read a whole book my first night on the train, I also slept thinking about how I would probably have a better sleep on the way back having slept on the hard ground in a park for over a week, and I would probably be so exhausted I would be able to sleep anywhere which did turn out to be rightly so true. I used my jacket as my pillow and unzipped my sleeping bag for a blanket. All alone, I listened to my mp3 player and tried to calm my excitement and anxiety. Not having much money I didn't want to buy anything to eat. I had brought some random food with me that I pieced together, a tomato, an avocado, and some bananas; I ate those when I was hungry and asked for a cup of water. I got salt and pepper packets, a knife and fork, cut up the avocado and tomato, sprinkled some salt and pepper on it and ate it like it was a steak, my vegan steak. I wondered if or what I would be able to eat at Occupy Wall Street, and what would be vegan? The whole night in and out of sleep, the whole day milling around the train, going from the lounge, my seat, the bathroom, and into the night again.

The train pulled into Penn station at close to one in the morning on a Monday, or shall I say, early Tuesday morning. I somehow thought that as we got closer to NYC I would run into other people heading to Occupy Wall Street like me. The place was dead and I did not know how to get to Wall Street, the only people I could see around were police, I didn't want to ask them, but what choice did I have, I didn't see anyone else to ask, and wouldn't they know how to get there? I finally just had to after walking around a while longer, but finding no one else. I walked up to a set of them; they each told me a different way, and the little I did know about NY, both the wrong way. I knew they were going to take that approach, but I had to keep asking to try to get the right way. They just kept on playing dumb and asking me why I wanted to go there anyway and didn't tell me the right way so I was right back where I started.

Eventually I did run into people who must have noticed I looked out of place, must have noticed I had a backpack and a sleeping bag and they asked me if I was going to Occupy Wall Street? "Yes" I said, they said " I would love it, they had been", they gave me directions, but even better than that as we were getting closer to the exit on the subway one of the kids left his friends and told them he would take me there himself. I thanked the volunteer who guided me to safety. How relieved I was that I wasn't alone on my own setting out to find this unknown park to me, I looked up and around coming out of the subway to see the jungle of police and all their paraphernalia, you know, cars, buses, vans, scooters, flashing lights and sirens and such, intimidating to say the least. I was wide eyed staring around me at this scene from some movie. Lines of police standing before me for as far as my eyes could see, lining the several blocks we walked, and then we were there, the park was in front of us, my new home. The police were surrounding the park, it was dark, he took me inside, and then said good-bye, I was on my own, surrounded on the inside, I felt, by my own kind.

Arriving alone to my new home, so to say, not knowing a soul, scared and alone, with love, hope and trust in my heart, I moved on afraid, but doing it anyway, just wandering around, tired, not sure where I should or could sleep, people spread out all around me, some sleeping, some up, everyone a stranger to me. I finally found a place to set my stuff down, rolled my sleeping bag out and lay down, looked around and thought "This is the revolution"? And thinking it, it was in a questioning way, it was like, really, this is it? I hadn't known what to expect, but I think I had expected something a little bit different, at least at first impression. First I thought there would be grass, it was a park, I thought it would be a bigger space, but I put all those thoughts behind me for the time being.

I laid back, the sky dark in the distance, buildings brightly lit as high as I could see. The trees low right above my head, thin branches, golden yellow leaves, I breathed in a deep breath and rest. This was the view from my bedroom in Zuccotti Park.

∞

"An ounce of patience is worth more than tons of teaching"
Mohandas Gandhi

∞

Looking up on that first night, what a view, a little nature, a lot of city, I have always dreamed of living in NYC, at least for a little while. We, me and Curtiss, had talked about how much we both would love to live in the city for a while. I love the noise of the streets, the many people always on them. Never did I think I would ever really get my chance, the city being so expensive, and us with a house in Florida, but I thought maybe someday, well I was here with the cheapest bedroom, with the best view of the city. The trees, with their still green leaves, the black sky beyond, the buildings lit up the night, never quite dark, never quiet, always miraculous. I made it, alone, not knowing quite where to go, somehow I made it just the same, just like I knew I would if I just took that first step and kept putting one foot in front of the other. Now I was here, now what? What was this place and what was my place in it? Yes I came, but what comes next, it was so late, I was so tired, I had come such a long way and I made it, but I was overwhelmed and disoriented and needed to put a night of sleep between me and what comes next.

Not trusting anyone I didn't know, how I ever would, not knowing anyone, but it was for me to figure out later so I put my hand on my backpack to know it was there , used my jacket as my pillow so no one could take it and I closed my eyes and slept. I woke in the middle of the night to someone sitting up confused asking if I saw his green backpack. It was gone, someone stole it, it had his medicine in it. I grabbed onto my backpack a little tighter. I never saw him again, but I did find his back pack in Mt. Laundry after one of the rains quite a few weeks later, it was green and when I looked in it among other things was his medicine. Waking up many times to put a hand on all my belongings to know they were in fact still there, then I closed my eyes again and fell back, taking it all in, the jackhammers and all, the noise never stopping, but I did sleep and it was light out one of the times I awoke and I had made it through my first night. I woke up to the bright morning light and looked around. It was lively in the middle of the night, everyone was now just starting to wake up like me, some still asleep scattered around in sleeping bags, on tarps, camping mats, cardboard, air mattresses, and real mattresses randomly set down. Now, to that question of what next?

I was glad to see and smell coffee and bagels in the morning, too good to be true, I could wake up, walk up and get a cup? Trying to find milk and sugar, the only way to have a satisfying cup of coffee in my opinion, I grabbed an everything bagel, plain, no vegan butter, but I was used to that, granola bars, assorted to choose from. I felt as if I had it all. I was here; I had food, a place to sleep. The bathroom was the next question. McDonalds, the answer everyone told everyone, I hardly heard anyone tell a different place, although there were different places people went. The line was long, but it was available so I waited and was glad for it. I had to carry everything around with me, this could get annoying, I didn't want to do it, but how would it be any other way when I didn't know anyone?

Joey must have seen it was my first day, for after I got acquainted with the place I could tell the people whose first day it was too, just by the look in their eyes, the look of a dazed individual. He reached out to me, sitting on an overturned bucket he used for a stool, smiling, introducing himself as "Joey from Cincinnati", with a big smile and a sense of humor, he asked me to sit down and we got to know each other a little. He talked about how he holds down the camp during the day, watches people's stuff so nothing gets stolen, he pointed out an area right by the tree next to where he was sitting that held all the people's stuff, he said he would watch my stuff too, he was going to be there anyway, he was the one that stayed and held the camp, he would be there if I needed anything. The first person in which I would trust, I did bring my jacket even though it was not so cold out, I didn't want to leave my ID, money, ticket home, phone, camera, or my mp3 player with anyone, I wanted all that stuff to stay on me so there was no question it was safe.

With my bulky, heavy load set down I could explore a little more, at first I didn't go very far, not really knowing this person and not trusting too easily, especially of strangers, but every time I went back he was there and so was all my stuff so I started feeling less anxious about it and stretched out a little further still to the outskirts of the park, checking out all there was to see, reading the signs people were holding standing in a line and the signs people had placed on the ground, going to all the different areas of activity; the library, tobacco table, sanitation, sustainability, arts and culture, drums, signs, empathy, info, media, press, kitchen, asking questions, finding little answers, I don't mean no answers, I literally mean little answers, so I asked more questions. Little by little I started to orient myself to my surroundings and find out about the inner workings of this thing called Occupy Wall Street, this place called Zuccotti Park.

I heard a mic-check about NVC classes, the mic-check looked and sounded like this; mic-check, repeated by whoever could hear her, mic-check, we will be meeting here, we will be meeting here, for an NVC class, for an NVC class, NVC standing for non-violent communication, NVC standing for non-violent communication, If you would like to join this class, if you would like to join this class, meet here, she held a sign in her hands above her head that read meet here for NVC class. I loved this idea and wanted to learn more, Tashi as I would later learn her name mic-checked the class in the park, I met where they mic-checked the class and followed her to where the class was held off site. Tashi, a young girl , she came here from Germany knowing English well with a heavy accent, caring face, long dark straight hair, calming voice and personality, she was teaching. We walked what turned out to be just around the corner, one block down, one block to the left to Charlotte's place, only we got there and it was not yet open, gathered together standing outside the door we changed our plan, so we moved on to the backup spot and walked over to 60 Wall Street, an open, indoor, public space. We gathered the unused, white chairs from the tables around us and formed a circle with them, and sat down to begin the class.

I learned the basics which are connecting with people's feelings with the need that is behind it. We went through feelings behind feelings, No matter what someone is feeling there is a met or unmet need behind it. If you can recognize the need, by saying what the need is, it helps the person feel heard and listened to, you can connect with them and then try to figure a strategy to meet their need, in recognizing the need the person feels validated, in recognizing the need in yourself, you feel validated. It was a lot of the things I was already trying to do in my own life as a parent, a wife, a friend. It gave me yet one more piece to the puzzle, one more tool I could use, and for this movement I think it is an awesome thing to everyday have this class available for people to learn about what non-violent communication is. It is so important for us as a movement to be teaching this to people, not everyone knows and especially as a face to the community. The police listen in the background. They too are interested in what we are talking about.

I never heard the media talk about how our movement as being non-violent based. I never hear mention that we teach non-violent communication classes every day free for anyone who wants to take them. This is what the movement is based on, this principle of non-violence. The Quakers, Gandhi, Martin Luther King Jr. , everything I was learning about what this movement was doing, talking about, saying, the actions, I knew this was where I wanted to be helping and working. They had it all together; they had people united from all areas, living all the important points out with action. I spent years knowing there was a better way than violence and control of people, I spent years practicing it with my family and larger community, trying to be something more, more of what I'm not sure, I was so happy to be here, to experience this and to be around people who also felt there was a better way, a way that we can get everyone's needs met without controlling, but by strategies, and changing the strategies when one doesn't work.

What does non-violence mean for the movement? It means that we will not be violent in protest, even when we are being treated violently. It is a state of mind and I do know that everyone did not agree with it, some want violence, but as the voice of the movement it is non-violent. Through teaching non-violent communication classes every day we are speaking , we are stating where our values hold, yet everyone has a choice and we are not controlling anyone, control is where we are trying to get away from as a society, it is not working, people feeling as though they have no voice, we the people are not being heard.

After that first class I had found my place. I wanted to learn more and help with NVC. I felt it was one of the most important messages to get out there, one of the most important skills to share with people and I was already familiar with these concepts, but now I was being brought to a whole new level.

I went back to where Joey was sitting on his upturned bucket tied to the tree so no one would take it away, because if things were not tied down, they would disappear before too long. Hungry, I got something to eat and went back to camp to sit down and eat, taking a turn watching the stuff for a little while so Joey could move away a little, but he shortly came back and we could just sit and talk.

I wandered around to see the screen printers, printing shirts, which had sayings like corporations are not people with a monopoly type character and Occupy Wall Street with the ballerina standing on one foot on top of the bull. They had their tables set up on the edge of the park so people passing could stop and watch or stand in line for a shirt. It didn't cost a set price for the shirt, there was a suggested price but you put whatever amount you could in the bucket. Before long I had one in every style, my occupy wardrobe has started.

There were also the spray painters set up on the steps in the front of the park, they had all different cardboard templates cut out and you gave them a shirt and picked the template out you wanted on your shirt, they would get shirts from comfort to have for people to choose, much of the money these two groups made went to help support certain things in the park. It was a shared effort to raise money for the cause. People doing what they love to help spread a message.

Every day at five there was a march to Wall Street. I spent some time making a sign at arts and culture. They had paints, sharpies, crayons, which were all there donated for anyone to use to make a sign, with cardboard scavenged and hauled back to the park. We chanted, the drummers kept the beat, or we chanted to the beat, not sure which or a little bit of both. We marched past Chase plaza chanting banks got bailed out, we got sold out, banks got bailed out, we got sold out, up and down and all around Wall Street and the side streets leading to Wall Street, in front of the Stock Exchange, We are the 99%, We are the 99%, BOA, TD, HSBC and eventually back to the park again.

Outside of the park, on the outer perimeter people would sit and stand with their signs, one after another all around, I walked around reading all the signs, one by one, meeting the people, the faces behind the signs and standing holding my sign, myself, wall street, we did make a wall all standing side by side, holding our individual messages, which together became one message. And always the drum circle beating, and dancing on the opposite side of the wall and right next to the drum circle was the sacred tree of life, a 24/7 shrine, meditation, yoga, chanting, the stone man in his suit always sat there and the only surviving tree after the twin towers fell grew there, right in the middle of it.

The first night at the park I fell in love with the GA, aka, general assembly, a place where everyone had a voice, yes anyone who wanted a voice could go and be one voice in the many, I couldn't stay up until the end, but it was beautiful, it was something I was not used to, everyone's voice mattered just as much as anyone else's, it mattered not if you were a man, a women, white, black, purple, homeless, rich, or famous, even Michael Moore had to wait his turn in stack to say something. In principle it was right and just. The whirlwind of the day ended by the GA, a day seemed to last a lifetime.

Before each general assembly one of the facilitators would go over the signs, it was my first one, so I paid attention, your fingers up and wiggling for I agree, down and wiggling for don't agree, in the middle wiggling for I'm on the fence, pointer finger up and going up and down for louder, pointer finger just held up but still, point of information, both hands in front of you moving around and around each other was, OK move it along, I've heard enough, I get the point, you get the point, forearms across each other making a cross, block, your hand shaped like a C meant a concern, in using signs, you could express yourself without talking so each person talking could be heard, the GA was mic-checked so it had to be said in short phrases so all could be repeated by all and everyone heard through the magnification of voices and it was magnificent.

The second night there was a threat of rain, I learned how to wrap up in a tarp to stay dry, it was like a burrito, not exactly, but similar, one of the regular campers who would get up each morning and go to work told me how. Basically one tarp spread out on the ground with the four sides rolled up so that the water would go underneath instead of on top. The second tarp over the first and folded under with your stuff and you in the middle of the two with some small hole to let air in somewhere, my sleeping bag rolled out and my backpack to the side, this would keep the water flowing under me and keep the water off the top of me, that's what I did. The first night it didn't rain, I rolled up my stuff and brought it over to where Joey was to watch, the second night there was still a threat of rain so I rolled it out and fixed it up, that night it did rain and I had woken up many times to check, but all was pretty dry, a little damp, but not wet. The tarps helped to keep me warm since it's always colder when the rain comes. I was safe and snug in my tarp sandwich.

After the first rain my shoes got wet, it was wet for a few days, so they stayed wet, no matter how many dry pairs of socks I put on my feet, they stayed wet, they were so wet they hurt, I went to comfort to see if they had any rain boots and in my size, they didn't, but one of the many random acts of kindness towards me happened just then, someone was dropping off a donation to comfort and it was two pairs of shoes, I tried on one of the pairs and they fit and they were dry and I was so happy, I had never been so happy to get a pair of shoes, now my converse sneakers could dry out and I would have a dry pair of shoes, I got a dry pair of socks and my feet stayed dry.

The first two nights I camped alone getting to know Joey and all the other campers he was with, Rami, Noah and Lauren, but not quite knowing if I could join so at night I would find my own place to sleep, get my spot ready and it wasn't but a stone's throw away from Joey and the rest of the gang, if I popped my head up I could see them, they were right there just a few people sleeping separated me from them. I started sleeping at Joey's camp on the third night. I spent a few days getting to know everyone and I felt comfortable with them, I had built some trust to think I would be safe with them, safer than by myself, once I started sleeping at their camp, making it my own, they said they were wondering what took me so long. It started out with the four of them, and with me there were five, Me, Joey, Noah, Rami, and Lauren, there were others in our immediate area I also started to get to know, there were people all around, a big open concrete jungle of a park with built in benches, tables and chairs. Our front porch with turned over bucket stools, this is where we spent our time during the down time of the day and night talking to people. Spreading out on sleeping pads and bags along the floor at night, the space turned into our bedroom.

No plan of rain tonight so we could spread our sleeping bags right on the ground, no one seemed too organized when it came to where everyone slept so I just set everyone a place to sleep when I set myself a place, I guess it is because I am used to camping and setting up everyone's place, I took it upon myself to become in charge of setting up the area for everyone at night. I laid out the camping pads or cardboard, if we ran out and put down the sleeping bags so everyone was accounted for with a space on the floor. Everyone liked this idea; they knew they had a space to come back to at night, so until we got our tents set up and the space was already set, it was most nights my job making sure each person represented in our camp had a place also represented for them. Joey was the watcher of our stuff during the day and I watched out for everyone at night, we were a good team, everyone could always trust that their stuff would be there when they got back at the end of the day because of Joey and they could also trust that they had a place to sleep because of me, we all took care of each other in our own way, all different pieces of the puzzle.

Looking up at the sky at night from my sleeping bag, the trees, the buildings, the sky, I learned quickly to love the feeling of sleeping outdoors on the concrete in the middle of NYC side by side with people who felt as me, people who wanted a better world enough to leave their world behind for a little while for this world. I had survived my first few days sleeping on the cement with little more than cardboard for cushion; it wasn't as bad as I would have thought, and I wasn't afraid.

Without rain life was simple at Zuccotti Park, with the threat of rain, setting up for sleeping was a little more difficult, it made everything a little more of a struggle, keeping yourself and your belongings dry, especially things like feet and electronics, but getting ready for sleeping, I compare it to building forts with sheets and blankets as kids, it would be tarps, umbrellas, bins, tables, chairs, whatever you could find to build your tarp fort, with the challenge to stay dry underneath, inside. The park is built with a slope, so the front of the park is higher than the back of the park, the front of the park meaning the side along Broadway and the back side of the park meaning the side along Church Street, so when it rained the water would run down with the speed of a waterfall depending on how hard it was raining.

A few times we built it in a way to stay dry and a few times we built it in a way to wake up to rushing water soaking all, sitting in puddles, waiting for the day to begin and the rain to end so we could start to dry off. If we woke up soaking wet we pretty much were up trying to at least find an umbrella or a poncho, maybe some rain boots. Some days were bad, some days were better; all days were pure energy electric, thrilling, scary, terrifying, empowering, exciting, spiritual, indescribable.

I learned to drink black coffee, with the scarcity and unreliability of vegan milk and sugar I decided I better just not count on it and drink it any way I can get it, I learned to love it, I always hated black coffee, now I can't drink it any other way.

We made it through this night dry, by morning it was still damp, but not quite raining, it would be a nice day, the wind came and blew away the dark clouds and it was sunshine and blue skies and everything dried up pretty quick, for us that was, not everyone was so lucky, either they had lost in the game of tarp building or they weren't prepared, or didn't care and all their stuff was soaking wet and Mt. Laundry started to grow. In the beginning the mountain was not so tall, people volunteered to bring a bag or two home to wash and then back to the park to go to comfort to be redistributed, comfort even made a trip in a taxi cab stuffed with wet clothes to take up every washing machine in the place to help finish up the mountain turned to a mole hill, but with more rain came the mountain again and again and again. I climbed to the top once and started to sink into the mountain of plastic bags with wet smelly moldy clothes and quickly climbed down as to not be sucked in to the vortex.

∞

"Every great dream begins with a dreamer. Always remember, you have within you the strength, the patience, and the passion to reach for the stars to change the world."
Harriett Tubman

∞

"Each person must live their life as a model to others" Rosa Parks

∞

Sitting on our front porch, Joey and I watched our world go round. Our camp was directly behind the kitchen, the kitchen being directly in front of us, and the world of Zuccotti very much revolved around the kitchen, everyone passed through it, everyone, and they were always open, until they were asleep on the floor of it until morning to do it all over again, and the main volunteers for the kitchen worked 24/7, but at the least 14 hour days, even if you didn't see them in the kitchen that didn't mean they were not working, there were kitchens throughout the city who were picking up donated supplies and taking groups of people back to their apartments, where they would spend hours cooking and then cars or cabs organized to go and pick these people up and bring them back to the park with the food for the next meal and the next group of people and supplies off to some other location to work on the next meal, always making peanut butter and jelly sandwiches, washing dishes, cutting vegetables and fruits, serving food, finding water to drink and to make coffee, I met several people by way of always seeing their face serving me in line, or seeing them behind the scenes from my living room or bedroom, depending on the time of day and would walk over to say hello, to see how things were, the forever stream of people to the kitchen to donate, then that food being made into sandwiches, lots of peanut butter and jelly sandwiches, boxes and boxes of apples, oranges, bananas, granola bars, chips, hummus, carrots, pots of soup, then the steady stream of dishes in the bins to wash, volunteers being shown the ropes to help out with dish washing, the people on the line up to the table, the volunteers spooning a serving handing them a piece of pizza of their choice, pizza, the food of the revolution, cheese pizza, pepperoni pizza, vegan pizza, and the people in

between the dish washers and servers the ones
prepping, preparing the meal, we looked out facing the
back, where the dishwashing station was set up, three
clear plastic bins, one with soap, one to sanitize, one to
rinse, and between us was a path, the street, so the
kitchen was across the street to us, to get food from the
kitchen we just had to walk to the opposite side, and
from that side of the kitchen I was right next to
sanitation and it was here I stopped each morning, I
came to know and love this close crew, group, family,
tribe, of sanitation, each morning I helped them clean up
the camp because, well, it was dirty and we had to clean
it together. Lauren, Jordan, Dillon, Thomas, and Sofia
were among the core group, they were the life of
sanitation, and sanitation was their life.

Each day started over again just as the last, they
cleaned all day, all night, swept, took out garbage,
scrubbed floors, took out recycling, tied up cardboard,
bagged up wet clothes, sorted them, it was a hard job,
with little thanks, the hardest job, which most people
didn't want to touch, but I grabbed a broom and
dustpan and got to work, armed with garbage bags I
went around and filled them with other people's
garbage left for someone else to clean up. I cleaned as

long as I could stand, which was usually when I had sung myself out, I swept, picked up garbage, dragging bag after bag to the street, emptied full garbage cans and put new bags in and drug those to the street, picked up far too many piss bottles, empty water or soda bottles which now had a blatant deposit of piss in them, all while singing Wicked , as loud as I liked, not caring if I woke anyone up since people kept me up all night long, Zuccotti park never slept, and if it did, the jackhammers would still be there.

At the tobacco table I rolled a cigarette and stuck it in my pocket, I didn't smoke myself, but I took it to pass on to someone who did, talked to the guys sitting behind the makeshift table rolling cigarettes to their hearts content, I then went to find Thomas, to give him the cigarette if I could find him, one of the sanitation tribe, chocolate skin with short hair, a plaid hat, red and black plaid flannel and black jeans. I would find him sitting on the marble bench which serves as the entrance to the sanitation camp station, handing him the cigarette followed by a hug, and then I would sit with him a while as he takes a break to smoke. If I couldn't find him I would give it to Jordan if she was around, she had short sandy blonde hair and is always happy to have a cigarette and a hug and take a break to say hi, and if not Jordan then Lauren, and she always needed a hug too, so many hugs a day to keep the stress level manageable. They work hard and I bring them cigarettes to force them to rest a while, I jump on the food line at the kitchen and get food for them, lots of times they just go from one thing to another and they don't' stop to eat, so I take care of my friends who work so hard, building community, for we are all building community, every one of us, all the time, and in saying that I mean you too. Inspiring hard working people are easy to find here, bright eyes full of possibility, I see in Thomas, Lauren, Jordan, Sophie, all of my sanitation family, and not just in them, but in so many people I meet.

∞

"Live as if you were to die tomorrow. Learn as if you were to live forever. "Mohandas Gandhi

∞

After I had had enough of singing and picking up other people's garbage, then I would move on to something else, I was never in one spot for very long, the library was always calling my name and I would walk around the long rows of books, OWS in black sharpie along the pages marking each one, each one inventoried by the librarians, each ISBN# recorded giving them a record of every book come through the people's library, the people's library worked as such; you could take any book you wished, you could read it and bring it back or keep it, you could read it and pass it on to someone else, and there was no shortage of books because of this reason, people kept donating more and more books because of this reason, people liked the idea that education was free, everyone had access to it, with no strings attached, there were many librarians but Stephen Boyer was my favorite, a dedicated group and he was just as dedicated as the rest, the rest of the librarians, the rest of the occupiers in general who lived

41

in the park, and his love was for books so he spent all his time in the library taking care of it, some librarians ,Stephen one of them, going so far as to sleep with their precious books, the books on top, the librarians underneath, warm in their sleeping bags, doing what they love, their passion to share freely, There were poetry readings and book readings, Stephen worked taking people's poetry for the OWS poetry anthology book, so many great actions and ideas played out and all in the spirit of sharing knowledge and the love of books. Every day browsing around the books day and night, the librarians always there to talk to, to ask questions and to get to know, this was a community come together and we were all getting to know each other. We all shared possibilities of how a world could be, if only we, the WE, we believed in the we.

The library was in the front of the park, a large corner taken over by tables, and bins filled with books, books of every sort, every interest, concentrated heavily on politics, social movements, history through the eyes of the oppressors, but not limited in any way to these subjects. All the books were separated into their appropriate section, organized and reorganized.

In back of the library merged into media, those with computers, running the livestream, photographers, it's where the power was concentrated, where the generator was, and most all those in media also slept underneath the tables so they could make sure to protect all the electronics, everyone in every area worked their love 24/7 and all were needed, all jobs in this park were 24/7 work, eat, and sleep. The media then merged into info, which held all the information about the park, Occupy, and different issues within occupy, the schedule for the day, also they had a power strip for people to charge their phone, but it was still so hard to charge it, first there were only a few power strips for everyone's phones and if you used it you had to sit right by it and watch your phone or you might come back to not being able to find it, with the think tank sort of in the middle of it all, the think tank, nothing but talking about different ideas, different possibilities, but really I know nothing about it since I can't sit in one spot for very long, I would stand or sit and listen a bit, but I was soon on my way. In front of the library, up the steps was the anarchist table, which at first I didn't take any of their literature, but after passing it so many times I did start to take some zines and found, I could relate to anarchy, it wasn't what I had thought it was at all and so after I cleaned I wandered around collecting information, looking through books and checking every area out and eventually through the kitchen grabbing something to eat and drink, Peanut butter and jelly was a usual choice for lunch, but usually there were always other choices too, then would work my way back to our camp, and go sit down on our front porch and talk to whoever was at camp, which was always Joey.

I made 5 in our camp, but every day the number grew of who we considered part of our camp, newcomers, people camping close by we got to know, and we all wanted to join together, to help watch each other's things and watch out for each other at night, to become a family, our house, our neighborhood, our tribe. We consisted as a group of people come together as fellow Occupiers.

Our camp was named Sachsville, welcome to Hooverville with Hooverville crossed out and Sachsville written in its place, the sign was written on a piece of cardboard and although it was the sign for our camp we would grab it to hold on, take it with us on our daily march to Wall Street, or any other march mic-checked that we might join in, then we would bring it back with us and our camp sign would be back, marking our spot.

Joey was the main watcher of the camp, Rami, a writer and a waiter, he worked and he would come back late at night to crash, he didn't bring a lot of baggage, not even a sleeping bag did he have so I would make a space for him with any extra sleeping bags or blankets that we had so he would have some place to rest his head when he returned form a long night of work usually with some kind of food for us from his restaurant. He occupied while having a job as did Russell, working long hours for little pay, occupying out of the fact that he can't even afford a place to stay on the money he makes, more than the belief in what the occupation was about although he did believe in it because it had everything to do with him since he was definitely part of the 99%, working forty, sixty hours a week still with not enough money to pay for a place to stay, he came back to sleep next to Phil on his air mattress and later Phil's tent at night and always had a place on the mattress or within the tents thin walls. Andrew also had a job, he worked wherever he was on his computer so he could occupy while holding a job. He would go to wherever had internet when he needed to get work done and do it there, and once we had tents up, Andrew pulled his out and up, it was a junior size tent so it was short but still, if someone needed a space he would offer the tiny extra bit of space he had. We all came to this place alone, but found each other and now we were family.

Noah was 18, he brought his camera, he was there to photograph, he was supposed to take a trip to Hawaii, he changed his plans and came to Occupy Wall Street instead. He had his computer and would spend a lot of his time editing his pictures; his purpose was to document something he believed in. When we finally all had tents Noah was one of my tent mates, Noah and Rami, Noah was like one of our kids, we watched over him. When he was sick I made sure to go to the medical tent and get him Echinacea and Vitamin C three times a day so he could get better quicker, when he was feeling overwhelmed I tried to talk him down so he would not be as anxious.

Lauren was 35, he was from a catholic worker house in North Carolina, he came with the most baggage out of anyone, would leave in the beginning of the day, come back late at the end of the day and expect all his stuff to be there and taken care of, it was, but it was a challenge to drag all his suitcases to a dry place when it rained out. In the end I didn't think he contributed much positive to camp life, his piece of the puzzle was meetings, he went all day. He didn't come back on and off all day checking in, saying hi, getting something to eat and sitting for a while, he was just up and gone and never seen again until he was ready to go to bed, but it was from him that I learned of the catholic worker houses and I got to go to the one in NYC a few times with him and eat there, they fed people at the house every night, as many as the big dining area would hold, maybe about 60, some people lived at the house who had previously been on the street and they were somewhat taken care of by the volunteers, the catholic workers, they all lived together and those running the house would cook and clean and feed and house people, I liked what I saw there, I was seeing so much good in the world and finding out there are so many ways to give your life to service, the practice of peace and love and I was seeing possibility everywhere, hope everywhere, HOPE, helping other people every day.

I remember Claire on her first day, I could see it in her face she had just arrived, the look of disorientation, I was always looking out for people wanting everyone to be safe, so I called her over and introduced myself and the others around in our area and offered her a place to sit down and set her stuff down. I asked Joey if it was alright if she stayed in our area, I always asked Joey, he was first so I didn't really invite anyone in our space without asking.

I talked to her about how overwhelmed I was the first day I had arrived, it looked as if she would cry she was so overwhelmed, she did need to sit and rest, get something to eat and drink. I told her she could stay in our area if she wanted to, so it was she stayed with us and she was another addition to the group.

At night I would rub her back to relax her to sleep on nights when things were tense, which was most nights, sometimes, a lot of times; it was hard to sleep, to relax enough to fall asleep. For most of the first week I hardly slept, I was delirious I was so tired, It was hard to take a nap during the day when you didn't sleep all night, the park was full of people and reporters, photographers, people wanting to talk to you and you didn't want to be caught sleeping on the job. We all tried to support each other, take care of each other, make sure everyone was

OK. Claire came because she had lost her job as a teacher, she was on unemployment, she decided to come and occupy.

Almost right away from the very first day Claire started to sew a flag for our camp, she made me miss my own sewing projects at home. She cut up bits of fabric she brought with her, but got more from comfort, she was making a patchwork flag. She kept all her supplies in a plastic bag in her backpack. She sat on the ground in our area during the day and worked on it.

Sachsville was named by Claire, after Goldman Sachs and the old shanty town of Hooverville, so take the Hoover away and replace it with Sachs, the new Hooverville. Originally occupied in central Park, which we hope to reach by the spring, a taking of central Park for the occupation, right in the heart of the 1%, with plenty of room for all to come and occupy.

Comfort was the place you could go, anyone could go to get anything they needed, they might not have it, but if they did, you could usually have it if you needed it, or even if you didn't need it really, our camp had supplies from comfort, camping pads and extra sleeping bags and blankets, shoes, hats, coats, gloves, scarfs, toothpaste, toothbrush, anything and everything must have come through there at some point or another, I was not really attracted to work or help at comfort too often, I did get a lot of stuff from them, but it did bother me to see how selfish people are with things and how many things people want in their possession and mostly how people just expect, I don't mean to be negative here, but cleaning the park every day I saw a lot of stuff people got from comfort made into a big mess because it was just too much to take care of, and I wish they would take less from comfort, all that stuff piled up for a rainy day, and when it rained it would all get wet and be added to MT. Laundry, which was getting higher with every passing rain.

∞

∞

Ever since I got to Occupy Wall Street I have been completely alive, ALIVE, I don't dread the day, I don't dread my tasks. Even though I am sleeping on the cement, in the rain, in the cold, black coffee, hard bread, beans and rice, salad all the time, or most of the time. My body, my mind is ALIVE. I realized I did not need all these things to feel good. What I need to feel good is connection, people face to face, one on one, in small groups all uniting together to become one. Stuff does not make you happy, a quick fix, but not happiness. Only human connection can bring lasting happiness.

I came with intentions to change the world, in that, in coming here, I myself have been changed. A reason to wake up every morning full of life, no matter how good or bad my night of sleep has been, no matter how much or little of it I got, in rain, cold, snow, wind, my spirit still strong and renewed.

So from the first day I entered into Zuccotti Park NVC was a major focus of my studies, I wanted to be as much a part of it as I could, I went to the NVC class every day and would always learn something new, a new tool, I noticed after getting to know them and talking to them about how I could help that the few involved were too often overwhelmed and burnt out from the tremendous job and pressures of bridging the gap and mediating two opposing forces, two groups of people unwilling to listen patiently, openly to others, like they were willing and able to do. Also there was a lot on the plate of NVC, they wanted to run the empathy booth to talk to people about NVC and listen to them, show them empathy, but also teaching the classes and mediating, so I showed my interest to Tashi about taking over the empathy booth.

When I told her I would and wanted to take over the empathy booth she hugged me with open arms glad, relieved to have one less thing to weigh on her shoulders. NVC brought over everything to leave with us so we could take over the empathy booth, they had 1 table and a few chairs, flyers with info about Martin Luther King Jr. and NVC, a list of feelings and on the opposite side possible met and unmet needs, empathy badges for us to wear around our necks, a handmade sign which said Empathy booth on it and a donation box, a simply decorated shoe box.

We, Sachsville, set the table up each morning usually by ten or eleven am, and had it set up until it was dark, most visitors were gone for the day once the sun started to go down. So we had our permanent spot across from the back of the kitchen, step behind the empathy booth table and you entered into our living room by day, our bedroom by night.

Joey and Claire took most of the responsibility for sitting behind the empathy booth, Joey used his humor to entertain, inspire, and love people, Claire soft spoken, sewing patches together to make her flag, a lot of the day was right beside Joey, and I was always there for part of the day, and me, I would help sanitation in the morning before we set up, and spend time sitting with my empathy badge hanging around my neck throughout the day and then we would put everything away at night.

Day after day we sat and talked to passerby's, let them know they could talk about anything and we would listen without judgment to what they had to say, some laughed, lots cried, all loved the idea of giving someone empathy, simply listening to them, whatever it was which was on their mind and we didn't have much advice, we were simply there to listen, to listen with an open heart.

∞

"Any people anywhere, being inclined and having the power, have the right to rise up, and shake off the existing government, and form a new one that suits them better. This is a most valuable-a most sacred right-a right, which we hope and believe, is to liberate the world." Abraham Lincoln

∞

Possible Eviction

∞

One night Mayor Bloomberg came through for a hot minute plastered with foundation for a speed walk through the park, he started out at one end, the front of the park where the library was and walked the main path right down the center of the park, right past our camp, Sachsville, since we were on that main path, to the back of the park where the drum circle was, and it was like there he is, the mayor, getting a glimpse of him and then back in his car he went and drove away. The quickest appearance, he almost looked like he was quite terrified while trying to hide it. The next day there was a letter passed around the park, it read they would be coming to do a cleaning of the park. We took this as an eviction notice. We did not want them to come, did not want them to make us move all of our stuff from one end to the other to clean sections as it stated. That was a great threat.

We decided to clean the park ourselves. We put a call out to people for supplies and the supplies came pouring in, we had brooms, scrubbers, buckets, mops, dustpans, cleaner. We all were expected to help. The rain came, but we were happy, we didn't care, with every burst of rain we would howl, yell and laugh as we started to scrub all the floors from one end to the other. We swept up all the cigarette butts, leaves, papers, dirt, we planted new flowers in the flower beds, all night, with not a break, we kept cleaning, we took it upon ourselves to clean the park, it was our responsibility and we united to meet the challenge. The thunder and lightning rumbled and flashed and we howled, the rain came down upon us, soaking every last bit of us all, plastic ponchos were passed around and worn by most to try to keep something dry as we cleaned in the storm, it was raining like cats and dogs that night, and I say that because I think you can picture what I mean, meaning hard.

I was cleaning, playing in the rain; the rain was mostly over after 2 am. Lauren came to meet me at the park, Lauren being my almost sister in law, being my almost step-brother Russell's girlfriend; she took the train from Long Island. I waited for her sitting on the edge of the park. I watched for her knowing she would soon be there, I wanted to spot her as she came walking up so she wouldn't have to look for me, I saw her as she walked across the street, we hugged tight. I was so happy she had finally made it to the park and on such an important day. It was nearly 330 in the morning, everyone was buzzing around, we walked a few blocks to café bravo to get a cup of coffee and go to the bathroom, it felt exciting to be out in the middle of the night, I was wide eyed and awake, but tired, wondering how it would all turn out, glad Lauren was here with me.

We sat on the front steps of the park with a group of people while someone read the notes, cards, and letters people sent every day to the park, along with donations of supplies and or money, one after another from people all over the world, all over the country, all ages, all walks of life with words of support and encouragement, it was so emotional, in a few hours, any time really we could be pushed out of this park and sitting here in the quiet of the night, as quiet as any night in NYC could be listening to these letters, I knew we weren't alone, I wasn't alone, lots of times I have felt alone, I felt so alone it made me feel like screaming, Doesn't anyone care, doesn't anyone see, but here I was surrounded by people who did care as much as me about the injustice, the injustice done to people and to the world itself, and I was continuingly amazed by how many people did care, when it was OK to care about such things, they really did care.

People started showing up in support of us trickling in at first, starting a little after 5am, more and more people coming in waves by the hundreds, the thousands, they came; the park was filled to capacity, spilled over into the next blocks and across the street. They all came to make sure we did not get evicted from the space. It was absolutely amazing! They must have had to get up starting at 3am to make it over to here as early as they did.

A mic-check and black sharpies being passed around 212-679-6018, helping you out with the police state, we all wrote the number somewhere on our arm or leg so if arrested we could call the NLG, so someone handed me a sharpie, I wrote it on my arm then passed the sharpie on.

The drums kept the beat fast and anxious, matching the mood, anticipating, waiting, for what would come next. We started to hear that the cleaning was called off, but we didn't know for sure for hours, but then it was official, the cleaning was called off, they didn't come, they let us stay. We had been up all night now, the rain had stopped and blew out of town, yet again, everything dry and clean, drums playing in victory now, but the same fast and anxious beat, we would not be leaving today

All of the anxiety over of an eviction, our adrenalin crashed, Noah was the first to have a panic attack, from lack of sleep and food, and all the stress of the situation. We calmed him; got him something to eat and drink and I went with him to the bathroom. I was still nervous to leave the park for a second, worried that if I left I might not be let back in, or they might raid the park and I wouldn't be there to help protect it. I went to the bathroom at trinity and waited for Noah to come out, it seemed he was in there forever and I started to get panicked that he left without me. Noah came out eventually, but still I was the one having a panic attack this time. For me I suppose it was the same thing, being up all night, cleaning, not eating or drinking enough, being stressed about the possible eviction and all the noise, the drums so loud and so fast, the sirens, the police presence with their riot gear ready to strike at any moment, it all combined worked me into a panic. I had never had a panic attack before, but I know that's what happened, my mind was racing, my body racing and I could not calm down, I could not come down, everything just kept getting faster and faster and faster. I begged someone to lead a meditation so I could calm down, slow down, we gathered a group to join, we all needed it. We sat in a circle, breathed OM, OM, OM, we chanted, we breathed, then we played games to lighten up the mood and laughed, I felt better.

Everyone is overwhelmed with emotion and pent up energy from the impending eviction; it turned out to be a great day, filled with energy, after the rainy night. The people here were not like others, they were always willing to support people in need and I needed it at that moment in time to be alright again.

There was nothing to do but celebrate; we were still there and still strong, more united than ever it seemed. We marched the streets, we held signs all around the park, we danced, we sang and chanted. It was a roller coaster ride of a day, which ended with yet another hard to sleep night after a sleepless night, but the days were so full of energy, I was filled up regardless of how much sleep I was getting, eventually I would learn how to sleep in this place.

So I closed my eyes and listened to the sounds around me trying to sleep, the sounds of people all around, the sirens, the jackhammers, always, every night, the jack hammers. I closed my eyes and tried to sleep, I know I was tired, but after trying all night, I still felt like all I had done was keep my eyes closed, my mind wide awake, hyped up from the stress and all going on around me, and then the sun was beginning to rise and I smelled the coffee hot and ready, so I got up.

McDonalds in the early morning did not have so long of a line to use the bathroom, the perfect incentive to get up a little earlier than most, as if the coffee was not enough incentive, so that's the first thing I did when I got up and then walked back across the street for the usual coffee and bagel. I walked up to the kitchen, first the coolers with water or coffee, cups, hot water, tea bags. The table held plates, forks, spoons, knives, they would serve you from behind the table and you could go along and tell them what you wanted from what they were serving. Sometimes they had stuff you could take yourself like fruit or granola bars, the fruit was usually organic, usually donated. For breakfast they seemed always to have bagels, also usually scrambled eggs and potatoes. I always got the potatoes if they had them and of course my everything bagel. You could put cream cheese or peanut butter on it, but I usually had mine with nothing on it while drinking my coffee black. A simple breakfast, but how I looked forward to it each morning.

Knowing how important it was to keep the park clean, especially after the possible eviction, it was definitely the first thing I wanted to work on in the morning so after breakfast I turned on my mp3 player and listened to the songs I loved singing, songs from Wicked, Suessical, Rocky Horror picture show, Queen, I am still asking for someone to love, and still inspired by the words of Wicked, I am cleaning all the while, picking up garbage, sorting recycling from it, dragging it to the four corners of the street, lining the perimeter of the park, along with the police officers for pick up. I pay attention to no one as I sing to start my day off. I am sure I am waking people up with my loud clear voice, I'm not bothered if I do, I just concentrate on cleaning the park. If people talk to me I don't quite pay attention to them, I don't quite hear them, I pay attention to my music. I pass people walking here or there and police standing along the outside barricades to the park while I'm singing and dragging the big, heavy, black bags down to the four corners, I don't pay attention to so many people, I just sing my heart out anyway.

I had been there now for about a week and with the rain, I needed to do laundry and so did others in our camp, so me and Lauren, of Lauren and Russell, got the clothes together and started out towards china town to find a laundry mat, china town was the closest one, we each had a big bag of semi wet and dirty clothes to carry, and they were heavy, china town was a long way to walk with bags of laundry, but that was the closest place to go. I had barely left the park the week I had been there, only to go to the bathroom either at Trinity one block to the right of Broadway or McDonald's one block to the left of Broadway, or to a class at 60 Wall, or a meeting under the canopy of Trinity, or a meeting or class at Charlotte's place, one block down, one block over, everything in a few block vicinity, marches too, but still all around Wall St. So now I was venturing into the surrounding areas.

We stopped at Starbucks to rest, charge our phones, and look on them for directions to the laundry, as we were waiting in line for coffee, someone also in line asked us if we were from Occupy Wall Street? We both said yes and he wanted to buy our coffee for us, he supported us, said the guy with the suit by city hall. We were pleasantly surprised, it felt good to know, the second random act of kindness. After our coffee, and getting directions, we continued on, around the Brooklyn bridge is where the laundry mat was, just around it and we sat and waited, charged our phones, dried our clothes, folded, it was so nice to have all my clothes clean, then we walked back, getting closer and closer to the park I was more and more anxious to get back, wondering what happened while we were gone, is everything alright? Everything was fine and it was a nice sunny day.

∞

"Every Renaissance comes to the world with a cry, the cry of the human spirit to be free. " Anne Sullivan

∞

Before the park was an occupation, it had electric, it has electric, the park owners just shut the power off so we can't use the electric that should be provided, by every tree, and there were four or five trees in each row and at least twenty rows deep, there was an electrical outlet with two plugs, but the outlets didn't work. The first few days of the occupation they had power, but then they shut the power off, they who were the park owners. After they shut the power off, only then, did they need a generator, a few generators which were at first gas, then diesel, finally bio-diesel were in use, they ran the computers for the press and media, a charging station for people's cell phones, computers, cameras, a charging station for the media.

If only the owners kept the power already available, usually available to the public on then there would not be a cause for a generator, and furthermore are you aware that all the food carts surrounding the outside of the park had generators, in use, all day, just saying, well after a few weeks, after the failed possible eviction, the single file line of police walked into the camp, along with the fire department came in to take the generators, the did give warning ahead of time, but like I said, there was no choice but to keep them since that meant, no power, and no one was going to give up power. Stating fire hazard, a fire hazard created on account of them shutting off the power already previously supplied there, now they claim it is a fire hazard. Things are fucked up and set up.

But we are resilient and creative, and an agreement was made with one of the food carts to use their generator. We bought him a bigger one and ran a line where we could get power, so the police came and shut down the food cart. OWS helped him with lost business expenses and the NLG helped out with court and then we got bicycle generators. Days and days and long nights were spent holding flash lights to build and work on them running efficiently. It was sustainability who ran the project, also people from the bike collective, the two groups and the anarchist kind of overlapped some, as with lots of the people, not just in one group, but several, I saw Charlie working on the bikes day and night, people in sustainability never talked much it seemed to me because they were focused on some big projects and were in their own little world focused on solving these problems of the new society we had created in this 1 block piece of concrete, smack right in the middle of the financial district, not just Charlie but everyone's hard work paid off and soon we were running the computers at limited capacity on the bike generators, people would charge the big batteries and then those batteries would be used to run the computers and charge the equipment in media and then there were other bike generators with outlets to plug in cell phones to charge, people would take turns getting there exercise to help keep the charge up.

Water was another issue, which didn't need to be an issue, cleaning the park was made difficult without water, feeding people, preparing food and cleaning the dishes and the kitchen area was also made difficult without water freely available, which was something which was freely available except for the fact the management shut off the water to the park, for there was water in the park, in fact right by where sanitation set up their camp with the kitchen directly across from that, yet because it was shut off, it was another obstacle to overcome, try to do all these things such as cooking and cleaning every day with having to use big plastic Gatorade containers in a wagon and go off in search of water for drinking, cooking, and cleaning, go off In search of water access or approaching businesses and asking to fill up from their water source.

The powers that be always made it especially difficult when it didn't have to be and always we were threatened with the place being shut down for one thing or another. Really they let it go on for as long as they wanted to and until they didn't want to shut it down, it really didn't matter. It's such a game of chess, and we are all pawns, it's a game of chess in wonderland.

We went from sitting on buckets to chairs and plastic bins, plastic bins come along after the first few rains, before tents, they were to help keep people's stuff dry, we could put all our stuff in it and put a piece of duct tape on it and you could write your name on it with a black sharpie. Me and Joey shared a bin at first, but then we started to accumulate too much to fit all in one bin, so we pretty much ended up with our own bins, then bins for camping mats and tarps, extra blankets and sleeping bags, umbrellas. The bins became dividers for our area, the boxes were all along the two sides, we had a corner camp.

∞

"Every government degenerates when trusted to the rulers alone. The people themselves are its only safe depositories.
"Thomas Jefferson

∞

October 15th, about 1 week after I arrived, we marched at Times Square. Just a few days after the attempted eviction, the celebration was continuing. Lauren and Russell came for the weekend. We made signs; mine said "we will not be silent" I made it at arts and culture. Me, Russell, Lauren, and Joey headed towards Times Square, we took the subway there, in the park people had mic-checked holding a stack of subway cards for there and back, donated, bought with money donated, they were handed out to anyone in the park wanting to take the subway to Times Square rather than marching there, which a group was doing, but we chose to get the subway tickets and ride the subway there , so we walked to the wall St. Entrance located on Wall St., the 1, 2, 3 red line.

Just outside the subway station at Times Square we ran into Noah taking pictures, we walked up the whole street and still all we could see for as far as we could see were people and more people, we walked to the front down all three streets were people and more people as far as we could see, we were at the front and on one side seeing three other sides in a square, cops, barricades, the parade came down right in front of us, they wanted to get through, pushed the barricades, cops pushed back, but could barely hold them back, a motorcycle came through and one ran into a barricade, it seemed just to show off Police on horses, they told us to stand aside for an ambulance and brought through a police van, the horses bucked   up   against   the   barricade,   we communicated through the people's mic, thousands upon thousands, it seemed, 50,000 or more strong, the energy was electric, but we were all blocked in with nowhere to go,   we could barely move,   through the people's mic we announced we could go to Washington square or back to Zuccotti for the GA's, we had succeeded in our statement, we are a lot of people when we unite together and we have something to say, you better start listening, we the 99% will not be silent, we are going to make ourselves known, we want to be represented.

We headed back towards the park, by the time we got back it was dark and we waited in line for something to eat, it had been an awesome day, it was supposed to be my last night there, but earlier I had put a plea on facebook, I knew it would be hard for Curtiss all alone to take care of the kids and they would miss out on all their activities, so I needed people to help me, I wanted to stay, there was still so much to learn and they really needed me to keep things going in a positive way, I could do great things, I had waited all my life for a chance to participate in something like this, finally there was a group of people who seemed to care as much as I did about changing the world enough to try to do something about it. I wanted to be a part of it and also I saw how much I could help, I feel like I've just begun and I can't go home yet, so I hoped my friends would help so I could stay here for a while. I don't know how long, I can't say, I just know I want to stay right now and I feel it is important enough for the future of the world, a chance for change, who knows how far it could go, I want to help it go all the way.

I checked my phone and my friends were saying they would help me, I could stay, I was getting a positive response from people and if they would help, then I could stay, I love my family, It's nothing against not loving or wanting to be with them, I have a wonderful family and I have so enjoyed staying home with them and homeschooling them, watching them grow and now some of my kids are becoming adults and it's awesome every stage. I've been with the same person for twenty years and I am not looking for anyone else and that's just to say it and get it out there. I am excited about making a decision to stay to be a part of something that could change the world to more of a world that I want to see.

After today I was in awesome spirits, Russell and Lauren stayed the night, we had tons of people sleeping everywhere that weekend. The energy in the park was pretty powerful, there is no way to describe, the energy, the feeling, the atmosphere, this magnified throughout everything, everyone involved, everyone united, bonded together in this spirit.

The drumbeat all the time going, the heart of the revolution, no wonder the drummers had to keep a 5 gallon, no kidding, I was sanitation, jug of piss in their tent, no time to go to the bathroom, they did sleep, but then the jackhammers! And just a note that we could have had porta potty's, we wanted them, we could have paid for them through the donations we were getting, the city denied us, and it was only a short walk to McDonald's, and there were several places around to use the restroom, but with so many people it was a lot on the businesses, I just add this because I think that the whole story has not been told and media is misleading, government control does play a role. It seems some things are manufactured always to their benefit, to fit their agenda.

At night the sanitation band would play, Thomas played his washboard or tin can, Sophie her banjo, several rotating violinist's , right outside of sanitation impromptu nightly, with enough room for square dancing, and did you know square dancing is illegal, well that's what the police said anyway when they arrested people for it, yes good old blocking pedestrian traffic, another stretch of the imagination, but never mind, everyone gathered around, some hand clapping, some dancing, everyone enjoying the music, and this was a traveling show so around the park they would go lifting the mood wherever they passed through to end up back at sanitation and break apart, Sophie would wander around the park playing her banjo softly through the night.

Sophie was not only with sanitation, she also worked with safer spaces, just as the name suggests, a working group, working on keeping the camp safe for all the women who lived there, they worked on making anti-oppression classes available and also; what is consent classes, trying to educate people. She was also involved in direct action, as was I, and I would see her at the meetings at 60 wall and Broadway, and 16 Beaver and Broad. The night of the eviction she was in a neck lock, this means that two people have their necks u-locked together with a u-lock for a bicycle, and last but not least she was an unschooler, one of the many unschoolers I met. This was a thinking outside of the box sort of experience, so it wasn't unusual that there would be thinking outside of the box sort of people here, but I was still impressed by all the unschoolers and the way they conducted themselves, how they thought, all they could handle, it certainly inspired me and made me glad I had come around to the unschooling way of schooling.

From the day of the possible eviction to far after the march on Times Square, we were celebrating wins!

The next day was there was a rally at Foley Square, it was millions against Monsanto, they were protesting in all different places across the country today, I had wanted to go to D.C., before I heard about Occupy Wall Street , there was also one in Gainesville I was thinking of going to if I couldn't get to D.C., but I was here and so I went to Foley Square, I wanted GMO's labeled, at least, I wanted them gone, at most, and before Occupy this was my biggest concern lately, so we walked there, it was me, Russell, Lauren, a small group of us.

They had speakers since they had a permit, at the park we could not have amplification, we had no permit, so that's why we use the mic-check. I learned a lot, about Monsanto, their history, agent orange, but there was only a very small group of people there, maybe 20 including the people running it, they had a sound system, a table with information, and a petition to sign about labeling GMO's, we invited them back to Zuccotti when their rally was done and we all helped carry all the information and signs down the few blocks to the park, they were amazed when we got there, this was the first time they had been to Zuccotti and there were so many people there, we asked if we could keep the information and the petition so we could set up a

GMO table and they said yes of course, amazed by the energy of the place, so now we were not only free empathy, NVC, we were also the GMO information table, I loved that everything important to me individually I could help share the information here with all the people who wandered through wanting to know more about why we were here, I could talk about it, answer questions, collect signatures, Lauren and Russell would be there for a few days to help set things up with the GMO info table.

There were so many reporters and photographers from all over the country, all over the world, school groups doing a project, asking specific questions to whoever would answer them about why they were there , tourists, the flash of the cameras, people doing interviews, I lost track of how many people a day I talked to about why I was there. I talked to as many people as I could, I wanted to talk about why I was there, where I had come from, why I felt it was so important.

∞

"Cautious, careful people, always casting about to preserve their reputations.......can never effect a reform." Susan B. *Anthony*

∞

New York Post

∞

I have been at Occupy Wall Street for about a week and a half. This particular morning Rami came up to us at our gathering place, our living room, and told us how the New York Post wanted to do an article on him on life in the park as an occupier and he really didn't like the New York Post, didn't trust them, but they were going to do the article on someone and he was afraid who they might find willing to do it so maybe he should, but he didn't want to go alone so I volunteered if he wanted someone to go along for support. I didn't know the New York Post, but I knew some papers were more one way or the other.

We walked about a block away and had something to eat and drink while we talked, there was a

photographer there too, Kevin Facit was the reporter
and I won't forget his name I am sure, they both seemed
nice and interested positively in what we were saying, I
didn't have anything to hide I thought. I had been in the
paper many times, for things like protesting for peace
and the end of war, homeschooling, kids open mic,
theater, all the articles went the same way, someone, a
reporter from the local paper, The Beacon, or the
Daytona News Journal or Orlando Sentinel, whatever
paper it might be, interviewed me and from that
interview used the information to write a story, based
on what I told them, the stories were always positive,
highlighting something specific such as the topics I
stated, so that's what I was used to, people using my
words to write a newsworthy, positive, inspirational
story, there was never a hidden agenda, reporters were
always genuine as far as I knew, so that's what I was
expecting here, someone telling me what the story was
about, interviewing me and from that writing a story,
and really I was only there for support for Rami
anyway, he was the one doing the story, at first. So first
he talked to Rami, then he talked to me and I am who
they became interested in as far as doing a story and I
answered all their questions and let them put words like

forever in my mouth and make it something it is not, yes forever, why would I not be working to create a better world forever, lots of things were made something that they were not, what creative use of suggestions.

They followed me around everywhere I went and recorded all of it, I sorted wet clothes for a few hours and listened to my music, sat at the empathy booth and talked to people, went to a nonviolent communications class Jaya ran that late afternoon at 60 Wall Street, Jaya was one of the campers, not quite in our camp, but right there sharing space right next to us, he taught NVC, and also meditation, and spiritualist classes From Ithaca NY, he worked at a spiritual center somewhere up there, I talked to the photographer and reporter as I went about my day, walking from one place to another, explaining where I was going, what I was doing, how I felt about it, and so it went on,   and so they sent in a relief reporter and photographer in the evening, they followed me around to a meditation class, to dinner, the GA, then getting the camp ready for bed. I did the same things with these reporters and photographers too, these reporters and photographers didn't ask me as many questions as the first set, but they were still interested in what I was doing, how things worked here in the park and I told them about anything they wanted to know about, showed them around the place. Another relief photographer and reporter were sent in for the late night, I went to the medical tent to get ear plugs and vitamin C echinaechia to keep my immune system strong and kava kava to help me sleep.

It was hard to sleep at first, all the noise, all the time, not only were there people up, no matter what time of the night or day it is or the drums beating on and on into the night, but also the jackhammers all night long going on right outside of the park, literally, the road right next to the park, between Zuccotti and Brookfield. I didn't sleep or hardly slept the first five or six nights I had been there, I was only now figuring out how to get some sleep and getting used to it so I could fall asleep.

I woke up the next morning and everything seemed like usual, but then I was made aware of the article when camera and reporter from one of the news channels came up to me in our living room, where we were eating breakfast, I was sitting behind the empathy table, but it was too early to have it set up yet, we were all just waking up, and here is this microphone, camera and reporter in my face, " how do you feel about the New York Post saying you abandoned your kids" I took the paper out of her hand and scrunched it up and threw it in the garbage, that's what I thought of it, and, well I'm not sure what she said after that because I was just thinking, what the laskdf;haw;afhf;ahga;, that's what they are focusing on and then all that they said about trying to make it seem as if I am having an affair with Rami "the waiter from Brooklyn" I call him my lover as a joke now, I call him my gay boyfriend because that's what he is, also my gay best friend because that is also what he is. How wrong could the post really be and also they could print it like they weren't lying and it was true and without even thinking about the consequences for the people they were doing this too, I was learning a lot about this 1% and the power they have over the 99% because Kevin Facit and none of those other people who had everything to do with that article could believe it, but that's what they printed anyway and they didn't care because that is their job, just like the cops, not even putting much thought into if it was right or wrong, just doing what you are told to do, it's job, I understand it, I just don't like it and I think it must be hard living a compromised life.

They set it up so they can always point the finger to someone else, it wasn't the photographers fault, he was just taking the pictures, there were 2 writers for the article, Kevin Facit and someone else, someone else who it sitting in the office somewhere who I never met, so Kevin didn't have to look at himself being at fault, the other writer was the one, and that other writer well they could just point the finger up above her, it's so and so because they are the ones that told me to do the story, but that person just points up above them, and so on and so on, just like the police too, just doing their job and not making the decisions at all, it's someone else.

Well I almost always knew I did not want to be famous, scanning the sensationalized magazine covers while waiting in line at the grocery store, I thought it must not be a great life to not be able to go out without people hounding you, taking pictures of you and then using those pictures to say awful things about you later, and what about the families these famous people having to read all these lies papers print and have to ignore it, but still wonder I'm sure about the truth in it. I got my 15 minutes of fame in this way, I didn't even really know about the New York Post before that article came out, I did not know that it is basically like the national enquirer only people somehow believe what they say to be true, and people did believe it, not everyone at first, but eventually most people changed their opinion of what I was doing and there opinion of me in general, because if it wasn't the first article that did it, they didn't stop there, I found out who my friends were, and I didn't have that many, I always thought I wouldn't have to say a word about the kind of person I was, people would see who I was through my actions and if someone said something about me that wasn't in my character, people wouldn't believe it because they knew who I was, but I suppose except if the New York Post is printing it, if it's in print, it must be true, even my family didn't quite believe that it wasn't true, they thought, they said, why would they print it if it wasn't true? Are you kidding me, so me, who you have known for most of your life, you are not going to believe me, you are going to believe a newspaper, it destroyed a lot of relationships that I thought were pretty solid to say the least.

News and TV talk shows, gossip shows and such all wanted me to talk to them, newspapers wanted me to do an interview, people were calling me and all my friends, going to their houses, my families houses in

84

both NY and Florida, and at the park I was constantly being bombarded and now I didn't trust anyone, and Curtiss did not want me to talk to anyone, I did not want to talk to anyone, even the Dr. Phil show called me, but I didn't go on.

The next day another article appeared and had a huge picture of our family, my mom was calling me, my sister, my friends, just a few days ago my friends were supporting what I was doing, thinking it was a wonderful thing, life time activists some of them, saying to me now, Come Home, Come Home, I was not going to let a newspaper change my opinion of what I was doing, I was still here for the same reasons and those reasons are still valid and I could do this and it would be hard, but I still felt it was that important, the future depends on what we do today, so I felt I had to, I had to think of all the sacrifices past activists have made to carry on this dream, now it is my turn, it was synchronicity. So I still said No, I don't let people tell me what to do, I think Curtiss and my Mom, my friends, mostly everyone who knew me would probably agree to that, I do what I want, and it's all in love, but still, I think it's important for everyone to do what they want to, what they love, what they are passionate about, what they feel is right, what they feel lead to do, That's my philosophy.

For my family it was the same thing as me at the park, people hounding them, cameras, news, television, people calling the house nonstop,   the were on lockdown, so say Curtiss and the kids, it was overwhelming, I know with me it was, so for them who didn't ask for it, the media is cruel.

∞

"I believe in equality for everyone, except reporters and photographers." Mohandas Gandhi

∞

Not long after the night of the possible eviction, the medical tent is the first test. The tent goes up and stays up; the police come in one night to take it down, Mic-check to the park gets a circle of linked arms around the tent, Jesse Jackson shows up to link arms and protect the medical tent. The time is about midnight and I had heard nothing about Jesse Jackson being in the park, I'm not sure where he came from or why he chose then to come for we have never seen him again, but that night he helped us and was gone just as quick as he came, police leave without taking it down. I'm not sure if it was because of Jesse Jackson that they didn't take the tent down, but none the less it didn't hurt having him there at that moment.

However, in retrospect I see this as the beginning of the end. The cops don't take down the medical tent; yay the medical tent is saved, but guess what? From that moment on people started to put up tents and keep them up, their own personal tents, even when it was not raining and the tents kept going up, the walls.

Before that night the police would come in at night and cut the ropes tied to the trees, they would make people take down their tents if they put any up, they would arrest people if they didn't listen or if they gave the police a hard time about it, the day after the medical tent was successfully held other tents start going up and did not get taken down, every day the number of tents grows.

The people's kitchen makes a canopy with tarps above the kitchen, several tarps stretched above the kitchen tied with ropes to poles coming out of cemented Home Depot buckets, they extended over the kitchen and also some room all around so that if it was raining you could stand underneath and stay somewhat dry, and it's not just the kitchen, but media, info, the library, they had computers, cameras, flyers and books to protect.

Phil is the first one in Sachsville to put up a tent, Phil and Russell sleep in it, and if it's raining Claire squeezes in, the rest of Sachsville is still outside except in rain when we build tarp forts to keep dry. Soon there are lots of tents, OWS puts a call out for tent donations, churches donate hundreds of tents and soon comfort starts to pass them out, hundreds might be an exaggeration or it might not be, it seemed to be because they did not have enough to pass out to everyone, but SIS also did not bring all the donated tents to comfort, they held some back, how many I don't know, for reasons unknown to me, maybe for a possible move or another occupation started, also because they were not sure what the process should be to make sure everyone got one that needed one, also some of the people that worked at SIS were able to have first pick at some of the tents which were donated, it might not sound "fair" but I will say that it seemed every place, every working group, had their advantages, but those "advantages" did not come without a lot of commitment and hard work, so to some it might not have seemed "fair" but for me I saw that it mostly balanced out in the end, and everyone was free to work in any working group they wanted too, everyone from what I saw had equal opportunity.

Though comfort has tents, comfort has a problem, people want them, but they are not handing them out yet, because there's not enough for everyone and they are not sure of the process they should take, how do they decide who gets one, are there conditions? And there is conflict between those working there. That night was hard, comfort had to have someone standing guard watching the tents; even still tents were being stolen from behind the curtain.

In Sachsville Phil has a tent he "bought" from Modells, and by bought I mean got for free, so the story goes they were going to purchase it, but they were sent upstairs to buy it and then there was no one there, Phil and Russell walked out with the tent, they were prepared to buy it, they say, but it seems Modells did not want to take any money from them since they were giving them the run around sending them different places to buy it so they finally just walked out with it, some people had brought tents with them so when it was safe to put them up, they did. Soon after Phil's tent went up Andrew's went up too, Andrew brought his own tent, it is a one person, however he does invite another who needs to squish someplace, they never want to stay in his tent to many nights on account of it being a kids tent so it is not really long enough, but he does offer and on rainy nights someone always takes him up on it, the first rainy night was the breaking point for a lot of people with their tents, even though they had brought tents with them after the medical tent went up they still did not put their tent up because it was nice out, perfectly fine to sleep outside under the stars like everyone else, but when the rain came, the tents went up and since we could have tents up, most of them stayed up, few people took their tents up and down every day, at first we did but more and more people started coming every day and laying their claim that in order for us to claim our space we had to have our tents up so we didn't leave one morning and come back to someone settled in our area because it was a piece of clear space.

Soon after Times Square it started to come about that more and more people came to the park, not all of them as enthusiastic as me about the movement. Mentally ill, drug addicts, violent criminals, there were rapes and sexual assaults going on, drunks, homeless, runaways, gangs. It seemed no one noticed and no one spoke about it until the problem was out of control, no one acknowledged, so sick of meetings was I once I started to go to meetings about these issues, no one agreed, no one made a move, nothing got done, meeting after meeting, so that things got worse and worse still.

People afraid of telling people they can't be in the park, no one wanted to act like police, we wanted a better way, but had no real idea of what a better way looked and acted like with people who didn't care, even with people who did care, it was still hard to figure out how to create a different paradigm, to unlearn what we had come to learn, brainwashed to learn, manipulated to learn, about society, relationships, we were relearning and recreating everything we had ever thought we knew, but we still did not have it all figured out.

How were all these people finding their way to the park? Police would not help us, in fact they dropped off people just out of jail from Rickers Island a block away and told them to go to Zuccotti, free food and comfort brought a lot of people from the homeless population, the crusties, police would tell people they found drinking, using, selling drugs in all the other parks across the city to go to Zuccotti, they stood by and watched from the outside, never coming in to handle the problems they were creating, or helping to create as a tactic to destroy us and take our focus off the movement, to make us look a certain way to the public, to manipulate the situation. Hours spent cleaning every day, but to no avail, things stayed dirty and got filthy.

So pretty quickly our group, tribe, camp, had grown in size, once the tents got set up, communities were built, it was somewhat permanence, not sure if a good thing or a bad thing in the end, I know tents are necessary for the cold NY winter, rain, snow, so we were happy about tents since it meant we could stay and occupy indefinitely. We talked to the people we had come to know who were around us and worked out how to put up the tents so we would all be in the same place, people we knew and wanted to be around, all of us just getting to know each other, but still people we felt we trusted. We grouped the tents in a way where we would still have a common area where people could sleep on the ground and where we could have space to eat and live together, gather together and set up the free empathy and GMO info tables.

Sabastian and Cathryn have a tent that one of their friends brought for them to use, it fits 2, but they fit 3, Joey also shares their tent, but he says it is tight and he doesn't like to crowd them out of their space so if he can, he sleeps outside, in the rain or the cold he sleeps with them. Rami bought a tent and it is a 2 person although he fits 3 also, Rami, Noah and Claire or me. If Rami is away to work on his book, Joey will sleep in our tent. The first night Rami set it up and then went to work, he just wanted them to save him a space for when he got back, usually around 11:30 or so, when he got back that night Noah and Claire were in it, but they didn't set up a spot for him or leave him any room, it happened to Joey too, I would at first always set up a spot for him , but once he started to spend a lot of time with his friend Lauren, the Chaplain, I never knew if he was coming home or not, and I also didn't know if he was planning on staying with Sebastian and Cathryn so I stopped setting up a spot for him, there were nights when he came back close to 3am to find there was no spot set up for him and in this Rami and Joey felt lost, I started to make sure that Rami always had a spot again, but Joey was still a mystery, I lost touch with him and in that I think he stopped coming back and expecting a spot. One cold morning I woke up and came outside my tent to find Joey curled up in his thin red Marlboro blanket cold, I put some more blankets over him, I hadn't known he was coming back and I hadn't known he didn't have a place to sleep that was warm, we had a spot in our tent he could have used if I would have known he was out there.

Paul and David were in our group, but a little behind us, Paul and David were veterans, both of them had strong experiences, Paul told us how he was told to go into that house or building and kill everyone in it and there were women and children in the houses and buildings and he didn't want to do it, he started protesting then against what he was being asked to do, he was let out on honorable discharge, David was like a big teddy bear, Tall with a little past his shoulder curly reddish hair. Sara was from Canada, I met her on her first day passing by the camp while I was sitting at the free empathy booth and I invited her into our group, she brought a tent, so when the tents went up she had her two man tent to contribute, Lauren stayed with us when she first arrived, there were two Laurens, a boy and a girl, Lauren started getting involved with direct action and she took off, she had found her place and became heavily involved and she had her group of friends, we didn't see her much after that, she moved with the direct action group and camped with them.

∞

"Better to die fighting for freedom then be a prisoner all the days of your life." Bob Marley

∞

Tent City

∞

Once comfort starts to give out tents, everyone must lay claim to their spot. Now the entire park is occupied and more and more divided, by different subcultures and communities, class warfare, France, Anonymous, Sachsville, the Ghetto, the slums, the drummers, safer spaces, the people's stage, on and on and on and on.

Zuccotti became a microcosm of the larger society, every group represented in the whole. It was quite eerie. This microcosm was pointing out some very real and ugly things about us, all of us, we had to look at our own reactions to what was going on and see, face that we were doing the same thing the greater society was doing and we didn't like it, and we could not figure out a way to change it fast enough, to change our thinking, our actions, and it was hard to face and many people just wanted to put it back into the shadows so no one would see and we didn't have to talk about it, it seemed every problem whenever talked about had everything else tied together and so to change one thing we would have to change everything.

What was first described as the slums, even by the people who lived there, a step up from the ghetto, or what would later be known as the Jungle, was Sesame Street. A little more walking space than the jungle, filled with a lot more activists, although I'll never know for sure not really ever seeing the shadow people, mixed in the area which merged the jungle and sesame street. Also included in sesame street was Main street, this is where comfort, class warfare, chilligan, the tobacco table, the pet area, or the dog people, and anonymous lived.

I got to know and like and see the contribution from most of the people living in Sesame Street. A lot of the people just had nowhere else to stay, middle class America and upper class America were filled up, Middle class is where I lived, upper class was the area where the general assemble and the library, think tank, information, press, and media were. I put myself right in the center of middle class America without even knowing, I guess I subconsciously knew my place.

But because we did not want to call these areas upper, middle, ghetto and slums we had to find different terms. It didn't seem right to fall into the same patterns of thinking of things as we were trying to change. That's where Sesame Street came from. The reason being Sesame Street is in the city, on the city streets and it's not filled with rich white people, it's filled with lots of diversity and people who are struggling, not rich. It's a place where they are trying to make a difference, bring people together, and be positive, all inclusive, which we were this too, so Sesame Street it became, at least to our camp.

Sesame Street was full of life and full of characters, on my way down the path to medical I liked stopping and chatting with the people who had a front porch living room area to their camp, which consisted of two chairs, one being red cloth armchair where many a time I would be walking by and someone would be sitting smoking their pipe with a group of people sitting around in open discussion, laughing. Whoever was sitting in the chair would also mostly be wearing some kind of a fancy hat, playing the part. I'm not sure if they looked totally out of place or totally in place, surrounded by the greater park. As the weeks went on the chair became more and more battered and tattered looking, a few holes here and there with white stuffing coming out of the areas, but the people never lost their laughter or serious discussions, each time I would pass by and say hi. It was their home, their place to entertain.

Moving further down the line, the outlines of the jungle started to become clear, but did not fully materialize until after the medical tent, after the medical tent the areas eventually became a dead end, a no man's land.

On the Main street a fight was sure to break out a few times a day, people living here did not know any other way but violence, they knew they didn't want violence, they also wanted a better way, a better world. I learned it was just a few, it took only one to cause much damage, Once people knew I was on their side, I knew them as equals, they would come over and tell me, Chilligan found me at nick at night one night, he told me that Daniel had a knife and was acting crazy and they didn't want him in the camp, Chilligan and some others wanted to punch him, to fight him, but they also knew that wasn't the answer so he came to me for help. I went with him, he pointed out Daniel, someone I had seen many times out of control, on drugs, Meth I think, an evil twinkle in his eyes, the look of someone who knows what they are doing and loves it. We talked to Jean, one of the drummers, he was laid off from NASA when the space program mostly ended, so this is not a bum, just as the majority of people here, just saying, he helped us and got the knife from Daniel. After this, we were all watching Daniel, I told Chilligan to give me a heads up, Daniel started instigating fights with people, we asked him to leave the park, he refused, we linked arms and surrounded him, he laid down on the ground to fake a seizure, some thought it was for real, they were concerned, he was saying he was going to kill himself, we used that as our in to call for an ambulance. The police ended up coming in the park for this one, they took him out on account of being violent, but within a few hours he was back, so started my night of becoming a wolf, a lone wolf protecting the camp, keeping the liger out, for hours in the darkness of the night into the early morning I followed him, I was there every step of the way at every entrance keeping him out, vigilant, because he was bent on trying to get into the park, even more so because I was trying to keep him out of the park, It was a game he was loving to play, but so was I , I had come to like this game of cops and robbers we had going on, I got to be the cops protecting my people from the robbers, the robbers of their spirit, their soul, their energy, their resources. So as a wolf I stood my ground, blocked each try for re-entry, in my mind it was easier to simply stop someone from being let in to the park than it was to remove someone after they had got inside, so I circled around blocking every step of the way. He was violent with his words to me and used disgusting sexual language, got closer to my face, tried to kiss and touch me, but I kept him at bay and out of the park.

In the early morning an argument broke out between two protestors, I used this to my advantage to redirect their energy, I asked one of the two, an avid protestor with a fiery personality who might yell in your face because he wants you to listen so badly, every day shouting out at the tree of life his feelings. I asked him to take over so I could get some sleep, he accepted the challenge knowing what it meant and I told him straight up he was not allowed in the park and you had to follow him around in order to be sure he would not come in. I trusted him to be true to his word and went to sleep.

When I got up I was so happy and impressed. A whole group of people now were following him around, telling him he was not welcome, by this time he was crazier still, he was wearing no pants, with his jacket held in front of him, in his underwear walking around taunting everyone. A sign held above him saying "He is not part of our movement". Another three or four hours of this and us telling all that walked by that he flashed a little girl and the police stood still and did nothing, but then he was finally arrested, it took from the previous early night to mid-day the next day to get the police to finally do something. This is how far-removed they wanted to be, while surrounding us at all times, with their cameras, cars and police force.

As I said earlier Sesame Street went along Main Street, then down the road to the medical tent, after the medical tent you were in the jungle, I call it the jungle because you need to climb over, under and through everything to get around, every step of the way, as if you were in a jungle. There are no clear paths with many things in your way, tents, garbage, debris, people.

The people that lived in the jungle I never got to know, they were hidden within the confines of the jungle, in the dark corners. It seemed their tents were never occupied for long I could never figure out who lived in these ram shackled tent/tarp structures, they would come out in the night or I would hear them inside although I could never figure out who was actually living there. I would walk the area day and night unable to connect with them, find out their reasons if any why they were here and they did not seem to be contributing anything beyond chaos and violence, These are the people who in my opinion should be taken out, if only I could figure out who they were, they filled the area and kept others out with their jungle, unable to find a way out or in these areas were avoided by all except for them, which seems the way they wanted it.

Each day I would venture back there to try to clean up and make some sense, bring some order to this place. I would carry out bags of garbage and wet smelly clothes, along with the bottles of piss, buckets of piss, piss soaked cardboard. I would try to clean and sing while I was doing it to keep my spirits up in the midst of piss, of the mess I felt helpless to really be able to do anything about. No matter what I would clean up, I would go back the next day and all the areas I cleared would just be filled up with random mess again. I would work until I got so discouraged I would give up for the day. I usually would last about one and a half to two hours, at that point I was out of songs I wanted to sing and I would look around and feel like I wasn't really getting anywhere and I would give up for the day. Day after day I found it in me to carry on and give a dam about what the camp looked like though and try my best to work on a small area. In me doing this I felt as if others might try too to keep things clean, everyone would always comment on how hard I worked and they always saw me cleaning, some would help me carry out heavy bags or join in because what I was cleaning was the area where they were living, I would hand out bags to people who wanted to clean up their areas. We all need to do something is what I thought so I felt like I needed to do something if that is how I felt. I couldn't wait for other people to start, I had to just do it, and so I did. I know I did my part and I liked it because it gave me a chance to sing my songs, I was always in a better mood when I had a chance to sing in the morning. I did get tired of the same old songs on my mp3 player.

The circus, the Zoo, which starts on the street lined with cameras, a watch tower, police vans, cars, motorcycles, media vans, police officers, Blue shirts, white shirts, light bluer than the darker blue shirts of the blue shirts, homeland security, Brookfield suits surrounding the outside. Stepping in undercovers, they were inside and outside I'm sure, tourists, media, reporters, photographers flashing their cameras in the faces of us, the occupiers and endless questions repeating themselves, flashes and celebrities showing their faces in support or disgust.

Walking the paths, which grew smaller and smaller and ended up separating us, instead of bringing us closer together, as time marched on. Marching with handmade signs made from discarded cardboard collected from the street corners, spread out along the concrete, decorated with paint, markers, sharpies, crayons. Drums leading the way, inspiring us to chant to the beat, maybe we encouraged them to beat to the chant, maybe a little bit of both, we are the 99%, we are the 99%, all day, all week, occupy, Wall Street, all day, all week, occupy, Wall Street, All day, all year, we'll still, be here, banks got bailed out, we got sold out, banks got bailed out, we got sold out, all said in time to the beating drums. Drums, the heartbeat of the march, inspiring us to use our voices, we march on to Wall Street, visible to workers, the 1%, maybe?, spying out their windows, standing along the side as we pass by. Horns honking as we pass in support, passerby's holding up their fist letting us know they are on our side. We march.

My sign at the moment says "Be the change you wish to see in the world." At times I held other signs "Another world is possible", We are the 99%", "The power of the people is on our side", "We will not be silent", "Welcome to Sachsville."

∞

"Educate and inform the whole mass of the people…They are the only sure reliance for the preservation of our liberty"
Thomas Jefferson

∞

When I first arrived, the library was out in the open air, soon after the tents starting popping up, the library had a plan for its own tent. The money for the tent came from an anonymous donor. It was not just any tent, it was a tent make of PVC and Bamboo in a half circle fashion with a covering lovingly painted in the front with the words, The People's Library, the inside of the tent lit up at night with twinkling lights so it could still be used. It housed over 5000 books under its canopy, it was tall enough for anyone to stand inside and it was more a canopy then a tent, it didn't zip closed or anything, very inviting.

The tent went up a very strange way, well strange is a strange word to use talking about Zuccotti in general, but it was put up in the middle of the night, with lots of conflict because not everyone knew it was happening, they were thinking the few putting up the tent were attempting to destroy the library, even the people from the library didn't all know, so it was done under much protest, even by me at some point asking questions thinking this was a few drunks moving the library for their big idea, but it was done and when all was done it made a beautiful home for the library, it was already filled to capacity when built, there were so many books donated, I liked the tent, but it was also nice when the books were in wide open spaces.

Before the people's library tent the books were on tables in bins, during the rain all the books would be covered with tarps stretched over the bins and then the librarians would make their sleeping place underneath all the tables of books, once they got the permanent "tent" set up all the books were already under cover and the librarians set up tents right next to the library to sleep in. In the space of the library they would hold poetry and book readings, throughout the day and far into the night. You could browse around at books, the same thing, from the early morning late into the night. To me libraries are a calming place, and it was no different here at Zuccotti, no matter what chaos was going on around outside of the library space, when I entered into it, I could just go slow, take a breath go from one book to another, one section to another, picking up different books and getting lost in them for the moment.

From even before the generators were taken away sustainability was tirelessly working on the parks sustainability, but after the generators were taken away and the bike charging stations were the only form of power they stepped it up even more, they were building more and more bikes to power the park, there was a bike right in the back of the kitchen, right across from where our camp and the free empathy and GMO info table were, the bike charged a battery which powered lights for the kitchen, while the bikes several other places in the park powered outlets for people to charge their phones and camera batteries, and in other spots they had the bikes charging batteries which powered media and also lights in other parts of the park, like the library so people could still see at night. Sustainability had also begun to build a somewhat of a wooden shelter with solar panels on the top of it which would give more power still to the park, any time of day when I would pass by sustainability there were all sorts of people riding bikes to help with the power needs of the park. Sustainability was right next to sanitation and that worked out since many things overlapped, sorting the recycling and compost being the main two things. Sustainability also had an elaborate grey water system set up so all the grey water from the kitchen and sanitation could be filtered to be used again. They also worked on bikes too, since biking is more sustainable than other forms of transportation, people from the bike collective, times up, would help do maintenance on people's bikes. The park was a mini incubator. All ideas could be put into action, one big living experiment, and they had their hands full.

At night I liked being able to wind down and spend time behind the curtain in Phil's tent by flash or candle light and watch Claire sew her patches together, Claire would sit at the free empathy, GMO info table by day talking to people and sewing in between and Phil's tent by night sewing, this being her main personal project and contribution to the park, by this time Claire was mostly sleeping in Phil's tent with Phil and Russell and I was mostly sleeping in Rami's tent with Rami and Noah, but Phil's tent was kind of the night time living room for us, to get away from the crowd for a small while.

We maintained our safe space and stuck together. On the other side of the park, there were lots of people both selling and using drugs, and by drugs I mean more than just pot, staying up all night, fighting, carrying weapons, spreading violence, sometimes I thought it was an exaggeration, and at times it was exaggerated, but it is also true. I was in the middle of it all and I found I was good with taking care of trouble. I would say something and act, but most of all I liked walking around talking to everyone of all different walks of life and getting to know them, and then my job was done because when trouble came I could get in the middle and calm the situation down because they knew and trusted me, it's all trying to figure out a way to build community. At night became an exciting time for me, as community watch, I hate that name, then community alliance, hate it to, and then what I called community whatever, we at some points were called peacekeepers, I didn't really like that either.

Wearing a free empathy badge gets a lot of attention, suddenly people feel comfortable talking to you, they think you will listen and this is true. Walking around with my free empathy badge trying to get to know people in the park, they want to talk to you, they feel you are a sympathetic ear who is on their side so they open up, they discover I don't judge them, I am simply there to listen to whatever it is they have to say without judging them, I walk around and talk to people every day. If they are sick I bring them vitamin C and Echinacea three times a day, I just stop at the medical tent and get some for me and however many other people I am helping. This keeps me caring about people and I love it. When people know I care about them, they talk to me, they open up to me, they let down their defense and I get to know them and the people they are. The contribution they are trying to make, and even if I at first thought they were making no contribution before long I realize what an asset they are to this movement. They are doing the best they can with what they have and they have something to say, something to contribute to this movement. It is amazing to me, what I might have thought at first look to be drug addicts were in fact people that did support us, support at least a group of people, they are us, we are all in this together.

Someone who was in the area where the gangs were, he showed me a book of his drawings, me and him and his friends sat there looking through every page and they were amazing. He had drawings of people and things in the park that he had spent time on, he explained each one, and had I not stopped to take the time to listen and look I would have missed this artist.

Another kid who was very violent at times, I got to know him, he was mentally ill and I would pull him away and walk and talk to him, I would sometimes just sit next to him as he cried waiting for him to be alright again. He shows us a side of people we can't forget about, lost in the system, no one to help them, not one that cares about them, no one to make sure they have what they need to not only be safe themselves, but also for others to be safe because this is a person who can hurt someone. He told me every day he wants to kill himself and it's all he can do to go through the day staying alive. He thanks me for sitting with him, all he needs is for someone to be on his side, to be his advocate, this is one thing that is wrong with this world, just wanting for someone to do something so the dangerous people can be safely behind bars when they don't have to be a dangerous person, they can be a contributing member if only someone would care. He was not out to hurt anyone, just mad inside and has no way of getting any better, he also loved to draw.

Another boy always on the edge of violence, I got to know him form stepping in front of his many fights and trying to be there to listen to him when he calmed down. Each time he asked me if I had a boyfriend, he was upset with my answer of yes I have a husband. I listened to him and he liked it, he wanted someone nice to love him and listen to him, in the end everyone wants someone to love and listen to them. The world is a dark place if you have no one and nothing, anger builds up, little things set you off, the cycle repeats, keeps repeating all the days of your life, no one to trust, no one who is always there by your side.

Listening, I was learning, is a powerful skill. I loved my job as a listener. It taught me a lot about people. I learned there was something to love in each one, even those who seemed unlovable at first. It doesn't mean I liked everyone, but there is good in all I do believe. People are just longing to be heard and understood. They long for a place to fit in and to feel they are contributing the best of themselves.

At night the camp came alive in a different way than during the day. I called them the shadow people, the people we would only see once it became dark and late in the night. They would crawl out of the shadows they had been hiding in all day, the night was theirs. This is life like I am not used to, but I quickly became used to it and tried to get to know the shadow people so I could try to build some trust so I would be able to talk to them if there was a problem, They were just the same I found, there only flaw was their ability to handle conflict, or their inability I should say, quick to anger and violence. Volcanoes erupting all night we ran from one fire to the next and I got better at being able to handle them; I was able to step right into the middle of the volcano without getting burned.

I woke up to the sounds of morning tucked away in my tent wrapped up around Rami, with Noah on the other side, I couldn't tell exactly what time it was, comfortable, the sounds of birds and people coming and going, the smell of coffee coming through the tent lining. I get up carefully not to wake the occupiers on either side. I slide open the zipper to our tent and climb out, I unpile the bins to reach mine and gather my supplies together to walk the quick block to the church to change, but not before walking over to the kitchen to get a cup of coffee while it's still available. I drink the black strong coffee by small sips to avoid burning my mouth as I make my way to wash, change, and pray my thanks for this new day.

I wait in line for my turn, go to the bathroom, change into a somewhat clean pair of pants and shirt, wash my face, brush my teeth and straighten out my hair. I walk to the candles and light one, dropping in change if I have some in the little metal box beside the candles. I, always asking God to light within me the flame as I am lighting this candle, thanking him for my strength, courage, peace, non-judgment and asking him for more of it in this new day. I want to spread the love that he has given me to everyone I see, everyone I meet, so they will know god as I do, all love, no hate, understanding, peace, courage. I thank him for a bathroom; a quiet place to pray, food, a place to sleep that is still there this morning, undisturbed by the police, warm clothes, friends to keep me safe and give me comfort so I can make it through another day.

I leave the church walking back to eat breakfast and maybe get a second cup of coffee, When I first arrived, coffee was plenty, as I am hear longer and longer and the kitchen becomes overwhelmed with all the people they had to feed there is now not as much coffee, because there are more people and because the kitchen has almost given up on trying to keep up with the amount of people, they have now accepted there is only so much they can do and they can't please everybody, there is still enough, maybe there's only one big pot in the morning, at first I had a few cups in the morning, now maybe one, and one reason is because I get up earlier than most to get it. I really have learned to look forward to that morning cup to start my day. There's always bagels so I grab my usual everything, their day old, but still fresh enough, hash browns come at some point in the morning, eggs too, but I don't eat eggs so I just wait in line for hash brown, when the tray is gone it's gone, it is lucky for us we are looking right at the kitchen, we can sometimes catch them coming in so I can go jump in line to catch it when it comes, but still I don't always get them, but there's always enough bagels to go around so I've got breakfast either way.

After I get some more coffee and some hash browns I walk back to trinity for the 9am working group meeting. This meeting is held every morning under the canopy alongside of the church, under cover in case of bad weather although not quite indoors with tables and chairs set up. The church used it for Sunday morning

117

fellowship after church to serve coffee, juice and a light breakfast of fruit and sweets; also they used it for their lunches for the homeless twice a week. For this they handed out bagged lunches, some people sat down and ate right there, some took it with them, and that's about all I have seen use for this space so it was perfectly fine to use this space for our daily morning meetings as no one else was using it. The morning meetings were a check in of all the working groups, all the working groups that showed up anyway. We moved all the chairs to form a circle and all sat down. I was there on behalf of NVC, community whatever, sanitation and direct action mostly, these were the groups that I was most involved in, I could talk about what was happening in any one of these groups on any given day, whatever issues or news, and I would show up, listen to what everyone else had to say and when it was my turn I would give my report back for any information I needed to share about what was going on in the groups I knew about. I liked this meeting one reason is because it usually stayed on point and ended in an hour and I was able to get a lot of information on what other groups were doing, and what was happening in other groups, these meetings went very smoothly, we were making little decisions, I got to meet and get to know a lot of people from other working groups attending these morning meetings and they didn't drag on and come to no conclusion like many of the other meetings I was attending, it was a very mixed group of people who were focused on what they were doing, a somewhat of a highlight from everyone and I ate my breakfast and drank my coffee while I sat and listened to each person when it was their turn on stack.

After the meetings I could then talk to individual people about what they had to say, with questions, and also there was just the time to talk to people since it was morning and so casual and relaxed, then I would go back to the park and try to conquer the mess, and MT. Laundry was getting higher by the rain, it was now the entire corner almost of the park, it seemed, way taller than any man, and must have stretched about twenty to thirty feet and it was all clear bagged up wet clothes after rain after rain after rain and one snow and rain again, and nowhere was where the pile was going.

∞

"Whatever you do will be insignificant, but it is important that you do it" Gandhi

∞

Safer spaces women's tent was the first army tent to go up, on account of all the sexual assaults toward women. I had been involved in one, the reason being they came to get me to talk to the girl since I was with NVC/mediation/empathy and I was who was around, it happened in the early morning. I talked to her; I brought her to medical and had her write down her story. I wondered why it took so long to figure out that he should leave the camp, but it took the better part of the day. He was Jason's friend, and Jason saw that this could happen to anybody based on a girl's word and I was seeing that a girl's word was not enough. He saw it could be him and I saw it could be me standing on the outside of the tent making sure the guy didn't get away, waiting for someone to decide what should happen, me wanting to protect the girl and Jason wanting to protect the guy.

I was happy the safer spaces tent was going up because I didn't need it but all girls did not have a safe space to be and we needed to make sure they had one so anyone could come here. They would not have to be a risk of being sexually assaulted or raped.

It was hard getting people to move their tents around to make room for it. The people, who ran the people's stage came back to their area torn up, changed around with no room for it. It took them three days to get everything back in order and so was the same with so many people, if people were not there to move their tents or move their stuff, it got moved for them, many people came back with all their stuff gone, we helped as many people as we could try to track down their stuff, especially being some of the people that moved it, but some people's stuff was just gone and then we helped them get more stuff at comfort, find another place to set up, it was chaotic with all the displaced angry people over the few days. Something had to be done sometime though and there was no time when everyone was around so it was inevitable that it would happen, many people it seemed had put up tents although they weren't coming back to the camp every night, they weren't living in the tents all the time so the backlash

121

lasted for days with random people finally coming back after a few days of being gone, being very upset that everything was changed without their knowledge. Lots of people were on their own, they did not get to know and work with those around them, so when they left their tent there was no one to watch their stuff, we were lucky, we were one of the few camps that worked with the people around us and always had people from our camp there at the camp, watching, protecting, sitting at the free empathy and GMO info tables so this did not happen to us.

Our camp was growing still, we even kept up a guest tent so we would always have extra room to invite people who were just arriving to the park, and Eli and Elliot were two 18 year olds who at the moment were sleeping, occupying, the guest tent. We met Eli a few nights after he got here, he came to us in an upset state, the first night he slept in the park he stayed by the end of Main St, before the drum circle and he got his laptop stolen. We told him to come stay in our area we would watch his stuff; he wouldn't get anything else stolen. We were up all night someone taking watch, most of the time either Joey, Sebastian, or Andrew would rotate who was going to stay up when, someone until 3 or 4 am, then another one from 3 or 4 am until about 7 or 8. This way someone would go to bed early and the other one would wake up and then go to bed. They sat in a chair behind one of the tables or just in the front of the camp and watched, talked to people. This way no one could just come and sleep in our area without someone inviting them and also no one could open up our bins or look around and go through our stuff. Every day things were stolen, but most of our stuff stayed safe, lots of people were hurt, but our group stayed safe. We all helped out to make it that way. Everyone had their part and we all make it work together

After safer spaces was put up we had a new name we called our space, even safer spaces, we all made a great team. Right behind the kitchen we stood, there were many changes in Sachsville. When we first started out we just had our bags and sleeping stuff, every day we would clean it all up and condense it all together and then we would have a clear open space. Then Phil got an air mattress and he kept that up all day. We would sit on buckets and milk cartons or the floor, then Phil got a tent things started to get permanent, but still everything changed often. Next Andrew, Sabastian and Cathryn, then Phil and David, Rami, with Noah and

Claire or me then that tent got wet, everything in the tent got soaked right along with Rami and Noah and we moved into Jaya's tent because he was going back to Syracuse. The next night it was just me and Noah we had Jaya's tent to use, I spent hours drying out the tent and putting insulation underneath it, getting blankets and sleeping bags which were dry, I got all this stuff from comfort throughout the day and getting it ready so Noah could come back to a dry place because he was really stressed out and down that day on account of his wet tent, his wet self and the cold wet day. When he was able to come into a dry tent and get under blankets that would keep him warm, it made all the difference for him, then that became me Rami, and Noah's tent and Rami's old tent became Adam and his girlfriends. Then Eli and Elliot, then back to an extra tent we always filled and then some.

The tents got moved around as time went on and so did the free empathy/NVC/GMO info/ and then a coaching table and a No Fracking table. Every time something was added it just was a little bit more crowded than before, our living, community space shrunk just a bit more than before, but we wanted to find room for everyone, space for everyone, it was becoming more of a challenge.

The front of the park is the last to fill up; soon no room for GA's to take place.

∞

Separation between the haves and the have not's gets bigger; even within Liberty square.

∞

∞

"I do not want the peace which passeth understanding, I want the understanding which bringeth peace." Helen Keller

∞

A clever way to make a buck, a sign reading "don't be that guy" by Salvatore one of the camp pot dealers occupying, making a buck for himself and the camp not sure what order, but I think probably him first depending on how the day panned out. The first Sunday his success reached $1500 in money of which he dropped a portion of in each bucket throughout the camp that was supporting OWS with lots left for him and coffee and hot chocolate for all that he passed in the night. He would buy twenty, thirty coffee's and hot chocolates and get someone to help him carry them around giving them to all the people working in the park, sometimes I was helping him hand out the coffee, sometimes I was on watch in the park and he would come around and fill my hand with the coffee or hot chocolate of my choice. He didn't always get black coffee so I didn't always take one, and sometimes even if it wasn't black I would take one because it was cold and the coffee was so warm in my hands, then I would

126

drink half and pass it on to someone, since it wasn't vegan. I just wanted to warm up a bit.

His spot is in the back corner on top of the wall at Nick at Night, this was one of the places you could go to get a cigarette, among other things I'm sure, right at the end of the jungle, at the corner or Pine and Trinity. They had one of the stone tables in their living/gathering space, whomever was sitting there was rolling cigarettes if they had the tobacco, that's one of the things Sal bought from his money spanging, spare changing, with that sign, there was a whole group of them that would work together sitting and standing on the high corner bench. Nick at Night was one of the messiest, filthiest parts of the encampment, I should know since I was there every morning picking up the garbage that I seemed to have picked up only yesterday.

There was a Nick at Nick at Night but that is not why it is called Nick at Night, it's a rainbow term, the Nick at Night has the tobacco, and that's what Nick at Night had, and if you don't know what a rainbow term is that is a term adopted from the rainbow gatherings, there were a lot of rainbow kids here.

At first I refused his profits thinking him buying off the working groups with his meager contributions, but I listened with an open mind his feeling on how he was personally able to help people at OWS, the occupiers of this movement and face to face. I slept on the idea and held his five bucks in my pocket, thought on it for a few days and came to the conclusion that it didn't matter what I thought, he was making a contribution in the way he wanted, him and his crew and most important is he enjoyed being the "Don't be that guy "name and face and he liked being able to personally spread around to the people, the occupiers themselves, make the camp a little more cheerful, put a smile on people's faces as he handed out nightly coffees and hot chocolate to everyone around. He indeed caught my eye with his flirtatious personality and Italian attitude. I thought he seemed a Goodfella and he grew on me as did so many other people who I wouldn't have given the time of day until I joined community whatever and stared to make it my job to personally get to know all the people in camp and what they were really about. People are only people after all doing their best to be the best they know how. It surprised me that I was right about believing that quote from Anne Frank about how people are really good at heart.

Every day I would look for his smiling face and he likes to play the game of trying to win me over. He attempted to save me when I didn't need to be saved at all when I would get in the middle of a fight because I am a woman who needs to be protected. I think he liked that I didn't need to be protected though. I think he liked the fact that I was strong and not afraid and was someone he couldn't exactly take advantage of and I didn't need him, but I did, I needed him to be on my side and to be someone who I looked forward to seeing each day, if he wasn't around I wanted him to be, I caught myself looking for him more and more when his electrifying personality caught me in his net. I was always attracted to people's personalities, weather girls or boys, it was there attitude, their energy, that caught my attention, people are so interesting and so many different kinds of interesting people in such a small place, most people out there in the world were not interesting on average, but here, interesting and different people were of course attracted to this place, in the middle of NYC, at this radical political protest called Occupy Wall Street.

∞

"So he rises up to the level of hating the system rather than the individual who is caught up in that system." Martin Luther King Jr.

∞

I hear people calling for support and security, that's the way we have if there is a problem and someone needs help, they call out loud or a group will call out loud-support, support, support, or security, security, security, this way whoever was part of the smaller groups within the bigger group of community whatever would go to where they were hearing the call. The support people were medical, mental health, NVC, mediation, community watch, security, safer spaces and then some I'm sure. It is dark, but not late, It's only dark because it is getting later in the fall now and it's getting dark out starting at about 430. It's probably six or seven. I walk towards where I hear the call and see the group formed, surrounding the area. I see five people holding back a big tall black man they can't control, as they were struggling to hold him back I was racing to where they were. Rich was one of the five, he was the community watch organizer, he set up the

130

schedule. We, me and him, had been a team many times walking around together on midnight to two shift, or maybe the two to four or four to six, we always rotated. I asked out loud if I should get the police, I looked at Rich; he looked to me with yes in his eyes, so I took it and ran.

I ran up to the closest officer I could find with the look of panic in my face and the sound of it in my voice, I told them we needed help, Help! I wanted to run, but they only walked slowly, like snails, like we had all the time in the world, like a walk in the park. I turned around and motioned to them to follow me with urgency of the situation in my eyes, face and gestures. They still only walked, barely walked, around the corner, down the sidewalk. I was walking backwards and motioned for them to keep following with my begging them to be quick about it. We got up to the invisible line, the invisible entrance to where they were forbidden to go, they wouldn't step over it.

They stopped dead in their tracks, said they couldn't go any further, I begged them "please, please" I grabbed the girl's hand, pulled her, looked into her face "please, please, help us". She wouldn't budge, she wouldn't help, I could see she wanted to, there was the slight essence of tears, a sad look on her face, sympathy, but she didn't move. I had to give up asking them to help me, that is when I knew, they weren't on our side, they weren't there to help us, they were on the side of things other than people. Their boss and their boss and their boss were on the side of the banks and the corporations. They were there to hurt us, to let us hurt each other inside our park, then fault us. We did our best to combat what was thrown in at us.

I left the two officers standing there and ran to where they were still trying to take care of the situation; eventually Kelly had calmed him down, and in turn had calmed down the situation. Kelly was big black transgender person, she was one of the three women, one being me and the other Kim, who took care of most of the problems of the park along with lots of others, but somehow, one of us was always heavily involved.

She walked off with the guy and his friend, alone, so I followed, tried to get others, but they wouldn't. I wanted to make sure nothing happened to Kelly so I followed by myself far enough away to keep an eye on Kelly and the two guys without them having to notice.

She got the box cutter from him that he used to slash some tents, he left the park on to the subway with his friend and was walked their by me and Kelly, within the same night they were back and let back in the park, so it goes.

This was one of the ones we had to watch, although liked and getting along as long as everything was going his way, but he would always cause a problem eventually. The next time we had to tell him to get out of the park was also a time when we could not follow through with removing someone from the park. We would all agree with it at our "peace council" meeting, people from support, mental health, medical, community alliance, community watch, security, we would come together and talk about what happened and decide whether or not this person needed to be removed from the park. It was always due to a physically violent act, but there was always a grey area and people were not sure and so we decided anyway that what he did was a violent act and what we decided was if it was a violent act they could not be in the park, yet when we go up to him and tell him this and people start telling their side and then people aren't sure, they back down and then there are not enough people to make it possible to get this person out of the park.

We did come up with a solution although we never got to try it out because we were evicted from the park, but I had talked to DA and we talked about them being always available to get up and help us remove someone from the park. We would surround them and lock arms and walk them out of the park, people who were comfortable doing this could help. I also talked to sanitation, Thomas was on the night sanitation team and if someone was removed from the park he would help a team of people who were not comfortable with the direct action of removing them from the park, but who would be comfortable with helping pack up the persons stuff to bring it to them outside the park. We were starting to come up with solutions for taking care of our own problems within the park, just a few short months and a lot of issues are all of a sudden right in your face and you are coming face to face with all your prejudices all covered on the same block. You are face to face with government agencies, police forces, media, supporters and non-supporters, crazies, homeless, drug addicts, gangs, people just released from jail and violence. The prejudices we hold against gays, transgender, women, blacks, Hispanics, hippies, hipsters, young, and old, the whole of society in a block, but let's not forget about all the wonderful love and unity we all feel united in this struggle, this is what all brought us together to face these problems and try to tackle them together. Our world recreated all problems represented of what there is to overcome, we get to try it out and see how it works and how it doesn't, we have a long way to go and a lot to learn and still more to unlearn. It's like for as high as everyone got in this experience there were also the lowest lows, balancing out.

The next army tent to go up was the medical tent, and actually they had 2 army tents, one medical and one mental health, they moved them out of the jungle, because it was soon impossible to get in and out and if one had to get in and out with a stretcher, you just couldn't fit, so they moved them to the edge of the park, right on the corner of one of the main "roads" and the outside of the park, this way they were clear.

The army tents were dark inside; it was hard to see around when you were inside. Where the medical tent was before you weren't really inside the tent when you were there talking to people asking them for a vitamin

135

or some herb, you were talking to them from on the other side of the medical table and beyond the medical table were the medical tents, but now to see them you had to step inside, but it was nice and big inside, plenty of room for everything to be organized, that's after it was all said and done. It was a long time getting there. To even start a little further back OWS had acquired many army tents to make it through the winter in the park, and just to add this information, the guy driving those army tents into the city was pulled over and arrested for having a gun in the truck, I don't know any other details about it, so they were slowly picking and choosing what ones would go up, in what priority and where and what would be done with the people already in this space, many problems to find the answer to, but whose answer?

This time we are in danger of losing our space, we have to stay at our camp all day to hold it and stay together and we organized our space to fit our group of about 16-20 in the new space we have. Our physical space in the park never changed, we are always right behind the kitchen, and the kitchen stayed in the same place, but how it looked sure changed, this time we had to guard, "man" our space, all day, and keep talking to

136

them, them being the ones putting up the medical tents, and trying to work with them to keep as much space as we did so we could all fit in.

The empathy table gets pushed to the side during our "final" move. Everything just sort of got crowded out with tents, by the end so many people in too small a space, we barely have room for people and the info tables, we have to give up one of the tables and combine the free empathy and GMO info to one, sitting behind it you are backed up against a tent with not much space to move, but it's enough and we do have a lot of space compared to many people, many people can't even stay in the park because they cannot find space enough, they can't put up the tent they have because there is no more space to put tents, but we have managed to carve an area out for our group and have been able to stay together during all of the many stages, phases of park life.

And now at the medical tent the totally baddest Rabbi decides he is not going to move, he makes a stand, holds on to a tree, his arms and legs wrapped around it screaming and crying "he will not be evicted from his space". The mental health tent goes up right in the middle of where he is standing and he tries to put his tent up inside the mental health tent, which is a good place for him to be in my opinion. He is "occupying" the mental health tent, like in some experiment the tent within the tent housing a crazy rabbi. I am told anyone can be a rabbi it just means you went to so many years of school, I was wondering what synagogue he could possibly work for with his erratic behavior, a little like a two year old having a temper tantrum, but I have seen him be completely fine and rational, so I know that side too. Still people have mostly things in common.

After hours and hours of mediation the Rabbi finally decides that he will in fact move to another part of the park where the medical tent used to be. Ironically his tent is still inside the old medical tent; just now it is inside where the medical tent used to be.

Now we are between the medical tent and the kitchen. After the move we still have an area to congregate as a group in the middle of all our tents. They are in a long circle, more like an oval, with an area in the middle for chairs and bins. We organize it and it works, the only thing that doesn't work is the info tables get pushed out of our general congregation area. We

138

still have the free empathy/GMO info table alongside the street, our main street, but we are all alone while sitting at the table because of the way we had to set up our tents, so now it gets a little ignored. People don't sit at it all day anymore; we all still spend a little time there. I am mostly making rounds around the park wearing my free empathy badge now so I don't sit at the table so much, Claire does, Joey is with his Chaplain friend more and more I hardly see him anymore at this point. I miss Joey, he was once a rock for me and we were a team. He supported everyone by watching all of our stuff and our camp and I supported everyone by making sure they had a place to sleep at night. It was harder to do with tents; everything was not right out in the open so it was easy to see where everyone would be.

I found a girl crying because she lost her space, she went to the women's tent, but it was crowded, she was all the way in the back with her stuff on her cot and she couldn't get in to go to sleep. I helped her; I got her stuff from the back of the women's tent and had to climb over many girls to do it. We found a space, but when she tried to put her sleeping bag down she was told that it was a walkway so I brought her to our home and she slept in Sebastian's and Kathryn's tent, they were not there that night so she was able to climb right in and go to sleep and she was happy. I have been that overwhelmed before, usually it was when it was raining, cold, wet, weary, not much sleep, you just need people to help you so you can take a break and not have to worry. She had lost her space and didn't feel she had anywhere to go to just go to sleep. We gave her that for the night. That's why we gave the nickname of even safer spaces to our space.

My schedule was something like this at this moment in time, this moment in the park. One thing was, time ran differently in Zuccotti Park, it was slow motion, I can't explain it, but it was, so much happened in one day it was as if each day was a week. The mornings I would wake up, change, eat, attend the morning working group meeting at 9am, if I woke up early enough, so I should say, on the days when I woke up early enough, this is what I did, and the morning meeting was one of those things, meetings had times, sanitation did not so I would always do that. I would look for Thomas for a hug and a few minutes of conversation, Lauren I would usually find around and I would ask her for supplies, we would also clean together sometimes, where I would basically support her in whatever she wanted to clean, which was usually trying to clean out the really filthy areas, and tents and this was work with much conflict since the people that lived in these areas didn't want to clean it up, didn't want to participate, so in protest we would go around and clean and tear things down and get the garbage out, if I wasn't working with Lauren in the morning I was working alone, and walking from area to area of the park, saying hi, grabbing cigarettes on my way back and forth to pass out as I was around town. Rami also worked with sanitation every day so lots of times he would be walking around pushing a broom and I would pass him doing the same thing, or both of us changing out all the garbage cans around the kitchen. We also had our own camp to clean up and we did that too, swept, picked up garbage, organized the bins and stacked them up so there was room to be along with room to sleep.

I went to the areas of the spray painters, with their shirts and stencils and spray paint spread about and sat down, gave them a cigarette, looked at the stencils they had, and the shirts, maybe got something done, maybe not, but I would stop to talk, see how they were doing and be on my way again collecting garbage, bring the spraypainters back food, then back to sanitation for

141

more supplies, and stop to talk a few minutes, hand out another cigarette out, then check out sustainability, help them sort through recycling, drag out the cardboard, then back to collecting garbage. To the tree of life to clean up, sweep, throw out randomness, always being careful not to throw out any of the little pieces, books, pictures, stones, which were placed around the alter which surrounded the tree of life, the only tree in the park to survive 911.

I try to sit at the free empathy booth, I get a drink and a snack and take a break there, Claire sits there sewing on her flag. Everything is so crowded now, there is nowhere for anyone to sit if they come to our table to talk to us, all they can do is stand and it's hard to stop and stand in the middle of the busy street. We try to move it around to give it a better spot but it just isn't working, right at this moment we are no longer behind the kitchen but around the corner. I'm always wearing my free empathy badge and before long I am up walking around, checking everything out, from the library at the front, the Lego table, little tiny people holding little tiny signs, little tents, people gathered in groups, the kitchen, the drummers, all the areas represented in Lego's each day, screen printers, drummers at the back.

I sit with the knitters every day, they gave me some yarn and needles and I am working on a scarf. The knitters sit at the edge of the park and I sit and watch all the people pass. There are 3 knitters and me. They don't live in the park, they live in their apartments, but they support what we are doing so they come to the park to knit, they take the subway every day, bringing a folding chair to sit on and their supplies in hand. They knit hats, scarfs, even skirts, and they donate all they knit to comfort to give out or they make it for specific occupiers they have got to know. I make sure they get food by going to the kitchen and bringing plates back for them and me and then we all eat lunch together.

The food line is getting so long; sometimes I don't even want to eat anything just because I don't want to wait in that line. The kitchen is trying to figure out what best to do to keep everybody fed, they spend so much time just cooking and serving all they can try to do is keep up it seems.

They went on strike for a few days, so they could get a break, have time to meet, and maybe get some appreciation. One thing that was also bothering them was that people were always complaining. They didn't leave everyone with no food. They had peanut butter and jelly sandwiches, which worked out to be extremely time consuming. I hadn't spent much time helping in the kitchen so I joined them during this time. We made peanut butter and jelly sandwiches for hours upon hours hours, when you are feeding thousands of people a day that's a lot of peanut butter and jelly, we would try to get creative with all the different kinds of peanut butter and jelly and we even started putting crushed candy and nuts in it. One jar of peanut butter and a loaf of bread, another jar, and another jar, endless jars of peanut butter and jelly and loaves of bread. It worked out that that didn't work either. It still left no time to meet to discuss what should be changed. Some could meet, but others were simply making sandwiches all day. It turned out to be more work so after a few days, they went back to cooking real food. A few things did change, the kitchen now closed after dinner and anyone bringing food after that could put it out, but it wasn't the kitchens responsibility to take care of it and they had 3 meals a day instead of always having food out at all times. A few changes, but not much of a difference it made talking to the people from the kitchen. The kitchen was always busy and always in the need of more help, but the same with so many other working groups who were trying to keep up with the pace of the park, sanitation being another, facilitation another still, community whatever another one to mention, so I am sure with any of the groups as were other problems of the kitchen.

Concerning more than the kitchen, but most definitely the kitchen was the problem of Nan. She worked in the kitchen and was causing nothing but problem, she was voted out of the kitchen but refused to leave and the rest of the group was left wondering what to do now. It was not the only place she caused a problem; in the GA too she was constantly causing conflict/in fighting, these are better words for what her actions brought about. It was making the GA's unbearable for a lot of people; nothing could get accomplished because when it came down to it she blocked everything. We had a running joke that she even blocked her own proposal, and if she did it wouldn't have surprised anyone. The other place she was causing lots of conflict was the women's tent. She was also voted out of the safer spaces women's tent, but also refused to leave. She would sit outside the tent like she owned it.

Still even with so many people trying to destroy there were so many people who worked so hard for the movement day in and day out, never tiring for the spirit in them is strong. They realize there is so much work to be done and not enough people cooperating to make it easy for the rest of us who see and want to be a part of making this park a beautiful welcoming place, and example of how we could live.

I walk around the park talking to everyone and then head back to free empathy and my own camp, sitting at the table for another small while.

March to Wall Street every day, I barely leave the park except to use the bathroom and go on marches, day marches and night marches. At night we start to round people up at about 8pm or so and usually will start marching at around 9pm or so. The night marches were silent, except for the stomping of our feet on the pavement. This way they couldn't say we were being loud after the time when the laws said you had to be quiet. So we marched in silence, all through the financial district, Wall Street and all the streets around, I thought we sounded like an army coming down the street, with the cops marching right beside us, causing trouble since we were violently, silently, marching. The flag would wave and the masks would go on, and it seemed anything could be considered a mask, just wearing a bandana around your neck could be considered wearing a mask if they wanted it to be so. Marching was our way of saying, we have had enough, we are not going to take it anymore, we want change, we are not going to stop, we are not going away, all day, all week, occupy, wall street, is what we said and we meant it and marching all different times of the day, morning, noon, evening, night, we were saying this, we all know a better world is possible.

The arts and culture area was swallowed up by Mt. Laundry plus tents all around, there was no clear area for art. The next set of army tents would go up when me and Thomas hatched a plan to throw out Mt. Laundry, it had been sitting there for nearly two weeks since the last snow and at the bottom it was the rain before that. The clothes had their chance to be washed; they smelled like mildew, they were garbage. So me and Thomas set a time, if they are not washed by this time we are going to drag the bags to the four corners of the universe for the garbage. The time passed, we pushed each other to start. I probably was the first one to start, but he was right behind me, we were following through. Once people saw us some started to help, then a garbage truck drove up, this was our chance, they agreed to drive around and the police agreed to let them and he pulled up, backed up and we gathered a lot of people and we started handing off the bags from one person to the next and putting them on the garbage truck.

Then the few people who disagreed came screaming over. They could not believe we were throwing the bags of wet smelly clothes, sleeping bags, and who knows what else out. It is a waste; we can't do that, who told us? Thomas said "he was sanitation and it was unsanitary". I said "we were doing this autonomously". She said "it was going to be washed the next day, stop throwing it out". We didn't stop even as I was talking to her I wasn't stopping, the stuff was disgusting, no one should be using it or washing it, it was garbage. If they wanted it washed they had plenty of time to do it.

The next day they put up two army tents where Mt. Laundry once stood, one the direct action tent and I don't' remember what the other one was, they were having much conflict deciding what the next one would be, where the priorities were. Those were the last two army tents to go up before they all came tumbling down.

∞

"I have learned over the years that when one's mind is made up, this diminishes fear; knowing what must be done does away with fear" Rosa Parks

∞

"Don't be that guy" Salvatore, the weed dealer from Nick at night gave me a bowl and some smoke; he just found out that I did in fact smoke. I brought it and some hot chocolate to Phil, Russell and Claire. I went around with Sal handing out hot chocolate to people in the camp, then went back to my own camp. We were in Phil's tent a little bit, talking while I was taking a break from walking around the camp. I had taken a nap from nine till midnight so I could be up for a few hours in the middle of the night as community whatever.

I unzipped the tent and got out after a very short time because I am the type that has to keep moving, I can't stay in the same place or do the same thing for too long most of the time. I went to find Sal to give him back his paraphernalia and walk around on Community whatever....

I saw bright lights and police, lots of police, in riot gear, walking up to the park, and I knew we were getting raided. I ran back to our tent community of Sachsville and told everyone it was a raid, I was nervous of course, everyone was, we fumbled around trying to decide if we should stay or go, ultimately it was up to each individual to decide and it was something to think about, even if you thought about it hypothetically, because now it was real, it was happening, so what are you gonna do? Stay or go? Stay or go? What should I bring? What do I need? What am I doing? I looked around, all going through our minds at the same time was an instant of one thousand things and then it was decided. I was staying; I knew that "who is staying" I said. "Are you staying Claire? Phil? And "Russell, are you leaving"? "Sabastian, Cathryn, what about you"? What about Mohammed, Matt? Where was Andrew, Joey? Rami is working on his book, Joey must be with the Chaplains. Get your stuff together! What should I bring? What do I need? I re packed, but not good, I questioned what I brought, I had too much, but I didn't want to leave anything else, I wish I gave stuff to Phil and Russell to hold for me.

"Anyone staying get by the kitchen"! I heard someone I recognized from DA yell. The cops came into the park; they stood in lines with their riot gear all around the park, like storm troopers, line after line of guys dressed in full riot gear standing before us, surrounding us from the outside of the park. They told us to get our stuff and get out or face arrest. We sat by the kitchen, I tried to call Rami, he didn't answer, I texted him, we are being raided, again, they are raiding. We sat around the kitchen, while DA Ulocked their necks together in the kitchen. We sat in a locked arms position, some sat in caterpillar positions, about three people wide, waiting, watching them slash the tents, take them away, haul them into garbage trucks and dumpsters. They cleared the whole park out, every tent! And as they cleared the police in the riot gear advanced one step at a time, until they were up to the kitchen.

They announced if we do not leave the park we will face arrest. I had a backpack and a bag and my coat on, we were locking arms, the guy before us was punched in the face, hit with the baton, they pulled him apart, took him away. Claire they pulled, we held on as tight as we could, when she was pulled from my arms she went limp, she lost her sewing bag, I held on to it, they pulled me apart, I held on, but when they got me free I closed my eyes and went limp, it took four of them to pick me up, they put the cuffs on me, I was dead weight. They opened my backpack when we got to the street and dumped everything on the street, all that time sitting there locking arms I was so worried I didn't have my rainbow hat in my back pack, I thought I had left it in the tent, but I did have it all along only I was looking at it on the street now. I broke free, really on instinct, my hand cuffs must not have been that tight and when they threw everything on the street and I saw it there I just reached out for it and my hands were free, I tried to get my stuff off the street, they were on top of me pushing me down, putting the handcuffs on and this time they were tight, I asked them why they did that? They said my backpack opened, I said" why couldn't you have zipped it up, why did they have to throw it on the street"? It would have been easier for them to zip it up then it was for them to unzip it and rip everything out throwing it on the street. I didn't understand, I did understand, but I just didn't want to believe it. I waited to get into the bus; they took a picture of me with my arresting officer. Me and Claire were together at least.

153

That was a good thing that I wasn't alone. I had someone from my Sachsville family with me.

The cops took us on quite a ride because what should have taken about five minutes took about two hours. We just drove and parked and waited and then turned around and drove around the block, parked and sat, the handcuffs are tight, I can't feel my hands, I ask nothing then I cry, I just sit there and cry they hurt so much and there's nothing I can do nor anyone else either except... Claire pleads. Others are also complaining, the cop eventually helps me get my coats and backpack untangled and fix my hand cuffs. We get to the police station and stand in a line outside. Again we get our pictures taken, information filled out, our stuff was taken, put in bins set aside for later. We stand outside for a while in a line still in handcuffs. They eventually bring us in, walk the girls to one part and the guys to another. They inventory all our belongings, go through our pockets, and then they take off the hand cuffs and put us in our jail cells.

This is the end of the occupation, as the physical occupation in Zuccotti.

∞

Made in the USA
Columbia, SC
16 May 2022

60476471R10085